THE
BLOOD
OF *Favor*

THE
BLOOD
OF *Favor*

GLENN AREKION

DESTINY IMAGE® EUROPE
Via Maiella, 1
66020 San Giovanni Teatino (Ch) - Italy

"Changing the world, one book at a time."

This book and all other Destiny Image Europe books are available at Christian bookstores and distributors worldwide.

To order products, or for any other correspondence:

DESTINY IMAGE® EUROPE
Via Acquacorrente, 6
65123 - Pescara - Italy
Tel +39 085 4716623 - Fax: +39 085 9431270
E-mail: info@eurodestinyimage.com
Or reach us on the Internet: **www.eurodestinyimage.com**

ISBN-10: 88-89127-29-5
ISBN-13: 978-88-89127-29-2

For Worldwide Distribution, Printed in the U.S.A.
2 3 4 5 6 7 8/14 13 12 11 10

Dedication

To my King and Redeemer Jesus,
I love You more than life.

To my wife Rosanna,
thank you for being you
and a pillar in my life.

To my three blessings,
Lisa, Ethan, and Jodie.
I love you dearly.

To Mom and Dad,
thank you for your great upbringing.

Table of Contents

Preface

Throughout time, the world has searched for the keys of protection and redemption. Every type of ritual, performance, and self-abasement imaginable has been attempted in this search while the true Key has been overlooked.

The much neglected and noticeably overlooked subject of the blood of Christ trickling down the cross, which held captive His out-of-joint but unbroken body, is the answer that all of mankind has been waiting for. There are inexhaustible benefits of this uncommon blood; but before we can ever experience these benefits, we must first not only acknowledge them but also explore their possibilities. We are well aware that without the shedding of blood, there is no remission of sin (see Heb. 9:22). The power resident in the blood of Christ must be explored, then embraced.

We are also aware that *"without faith it is impossible to please Him: for he that cometh to God must believe that He is, and that He is a rewarder of them that diligently seek Him"* (Heb.11:6).

It is imperative that faith is placed not upon prayer alone but also upon the precious blood of the Savior.

Forasmuch as ye know that ye were not redeemed with corruptible things, as silver and gold, from your vain conversation received by tradition from your fathers; but with the precious blood of Christ, as of a lamb without blemish and without spot (1 Peter 1:18-19).

This blood holds within it manifold blessings because of the covenant which it represents, whether it is approached for the salvation of a loved one, forgiveness of sin, or when the storms of life come upon us. The book you hold in your hands will show you a step-by-step process to the victory in life that the precious blood of Christ holds. May Heaven kiss you and grant you its favor as you dig deeply into these anointed words.

Dr. Robb Thompson
Senior Pastor Family Harvest Church
President of International College Of Excellence
Chicago, Illinois

Introduction

Ever since I can remember, I have had an aversion to the sight of blood. At times, it has sent shivers down my spine. My first encounter with blood was when my granddad, a mischievous old sailor, called my brother, Bruno, and me to witness the execution of a chicken for lunch one weekend. At that time, I was six years old, and my brother was five; and we happily accompanied Granddad, not knowing what to expect.

With a cheeky smile on his face, he quickly put his foot on the chicken's head, took out his knife, and started cutting the chicken's neck. The chicken began squawking, blood was squirting, Bruno was yelling, and I became terrified as my granddad removed his foot from the chicken's head, picked it up, and threw it at Bruno and me. It seemed everywhere we ran, that chicken was right behind, chasing after us, with blood squirting everywhere. We screamed in fear as my granddad laughed, having the time of his life!

As I grew older, the thought of blood continued to scare me to the point that I hated even the notion of visiting a hospital and even more so the dentist. The sight of blood, my own or anyone else's, would make me dizzy.

Fortunately, there has been something else that I have always remembered as well—all my life, as far back as I can remember, I have loved Jesus. Even before I was saved, as a child, I loved Him. I loved reading my picture Bible and was amazed at the miracles He performed, especially when He walked on the water. I was simply fascinated by Him. I remember going to church as a kid and standing amazed at the crucifix outside the church. When I was later saved as a teenager, I loved Jesus even more and acquired a great hunger for His Word. However, even though I understood that Jesus died for me, every time the pastor would mention the blood of Jesus, I became squeamish. Then one day I had a revelation, and now I honor and love the blood of my Savior.

This book is entitled *The Blood of Favor*. The apostle Paul tells us that we have been reconciled to the Father by the blood of Jesus.

To be reconciled means to be back in favor with. Jesus' blood has brought you and me back in favor with God.

Favor simply means preferential treatment. Once you understand the power of the blood of Jesus, you will understand the favors that God has in store for you. The blood of Jesus is the blood of favor! We know that favor is not fair. Therefore, when you know the power of the blood, you have an unfair but legal advantage over satan. He possesses nothing in his arsenal to deal with the blood of Jesus. Satan will insist, "It's not fair!" And he's right. It's not fair...*it's the blood!* The blood of Jesus ended man's futile attempt to be reconciled to his Creator through works. Four thousand years of frustration ended with the blood of favor. The same will be true for you. A revelation of the blood is an entrance to a life of unending favor. It was God's gift to you and proof of His commitment and love toward you. The blood of Jesus is the end of your frustration and despair and it is your entrance to the high life.

I love the blood of Jesus because it is *satan-busting, sin-erasing, salvation-obtaining blood*. And the more you study the blood of Jesus, the more you, too, will honor and love Jesus.

CHAPTER 1

Power in the Blood

Wonder-working Power

There's power in the blood of Jesus. The old song fitly puts it, "...there's wonder-working power in the blood of the Lamb." Yet it would seem that the Church today knows little if anything about the blood of Jesus.

We suffer from a lack of knowledge for two reasons. First, our ignorance is due to the negative connotation attached to the words *blood* and *bloodshed*. Our 20th and 21st-century mind-set connects blood to warfare and terrorism. We see and hear through the media and read in our history books the negative aspect of bloodshed. Millions have died during two World Wars, and many other millions have died in other wars and conflicts since then. We have heard of ethnic cleansing in Eastern Europe, tribal wars in Africa, and gang warfare in our own neighborhoods; and millions witnessed the horrific events of September 11th. It is now a common thing to watch and hear of terrorism and bloodshed on our daily news. Satan has deviously used the shedding of blood as a mark of division; yet in God's mind, blood is the means of reconciliation.

Secondly, we are ignorant of the real power of the blood because many within the Church claim that the blood of Jesus is barbaric, gruesome, and vulgar. Satan has cunningly devised a plan to remove the blood from the

Church so that he can defeat the believer. He has convinced many that it is more important to be politically correct and not offend people; yet this way has produced a bloodless and powerless church. He hates the blood of Jesus because it speaks of his eternal defeat. It is a rare occasion to hear preaching about the blood nowadays in the modern Church, and yet God's way has always been *the way of the blood.*

> *Then Jesus said unto them, Verily, verily, I say unto you, Except ye eat the flesh of the Son of man, and drink His blood, ye have no life in you. Whoso eateth My flesh, and drinketh My blood, hath eternal life; and I will raise him up at the last day. For My flesh is meat indeed, and My blood is drink indeed. He that eateth My flesh, and drinketh My blood, dwelleth in Me, and I in him* (John 6:53-56).

It sounds repulsive and offensive to be told to drink someone's blood and eat their flesh. It certainly caused offence for many of Jesus' followers who choked, stumbled, and turned from Him at this point. Still it remains—God's way has always been the way of blood. Jesus was in no way referring to cannibalism or vampirism because when He made those statements, He was still living in His body.

This Scripture has a spiritual connotation. We partake and honor the blood of Jesus by acknowledging His blood when we take communion. Jesus was referring to the Old Testament example of the exodus from Egypt, when the Hebrew children applied blood on the doorposts and lintel and ate the lamb. This is also known as the Passover. This was the way out of bondage into the Promised Land! The same thing applies to us as we step out of bondage into eternal life through the Word (His flesh) and the blood of Christ.

If you do not like blood, you will not like the Bible. From Genesis to Revelation, the Bible is filled with blood, and most precious of all—the blood of Jesus, the spotless Lamb of God. The shedding of Jesus' blood was ruthless and unappealing to the natural eye, yet it was the greatest expression of God's love for us. As a believer who desires to walk in victory, you need a revelation of the power in the blood of Jesus. The blood of Jesus is the blood of eternal life.

> *For the life of the flesh is in the blood: and I have given it to you upon the altar to make an atonement for your souls: for it is the blood that maketh an atonement for the soul* (Leviticus 17:11).

But now in Christ Jesus ye who sometimes were far off are made nigh by the blood of Christ (Ephesians 2:13).

...and without shedding of blood is no remission (Hebrews 9:22).

*Thus saith the Lord, Stand ye in the ways, and see, and ask for **the old paths, where is the good way, and walk therein, and ye shall find rest for your souls.** But they said, We will not walk therein* (Jeremiah 6:16).

From Time Past

From the beginning God showed us His way—the way of the blood. Because it is the old way, many today consider it primitive; nevertheless, it is the God-ordained way. Through the prophet Isaiah, God says, *"Remember the former things of old: for I am God, and there is none else; I am God, and there is none like Me, declaring the end from the beginning, and from ancient times the things that are not yet done, saying, My counsel shall stand, and I will do all My pleasure"* (Isa. 46:9-10). There is an old saying—if you look to the past, you can predict the future. Looking back to the Book of Genesis, we can see how the future will unfold. From the Book of beginnings, God gives us a picture of how everything will come to be.

*And the eyes of them both were opened, and they knew that they were naked; and **they sewed fig leaves together, and made themselves aprons*** (Genesis 3:7).

Unto Adam also and to his wife did the Lord God make coats of skins, and clothed them (Genesis 3:21).

God made leather clothing for Adam and his wife and dressed them (Genesis 3:21 MSG).

God made this clothing right after the sin and fall of man in Eden. This account in Genesis 3:21 presents the first picture of what it would take to redeem man. Adam had just committed high treason and was attempting to cover himself and Eve with fig leaves. Then when God came to talk to them in the cool of the day, notice that God did not acknowledge their covering. God Himself took the responsibility to make a covering for fallen humanity. The verses above reveal *five powerful truths* to remember.

1. *God is the author of salvation, and He does not accept fallen man's attempt of covering.*

Salvation and redemption can be instigated only by God. Religion is man's attempt to cover himself. All religion is a futile attempt to cover man's shame and nakedness, but it is very clear from the beginning that God has never accepted religion nor will He accept it now. You cannot create your own covering. Man's deeds or good works do not meet the high demands of salvation. The great prophet Isaiah knew this as he wrote, *"I will greatly rejoice in the Lord, my soul shall be joyful in my God; for He hath clothed me with the garments of salvation, He hath covered me with the robe of righteousness... "* (Isa. 61:10). The apostle John also in his revelation on the island of Patmos emphatically reveals, *"Salvation [belongs] to our God..."* (Rev. 7:10). Only God can save us. As John so famously penned, *"For God so loved the world, that He gave His only begotten Son, that whosoever believeth in Him should not perish, but have everlasting life"* (John 3:16). It is not within the power and means of fallen man to redeem or rescue himself.

Really! **There's no such thing as self-rescue**, *pulling yourself up by your bootstraps.* **The cost of rescue is beyond our means**, *and even then it doesn't guarantee Life forever, or insurance against the Black Hole* (Psalm 49:7-9 MSG, emphasis added).

Angels could not redeem man and fallen man could not redeem himself as he was corrupted with sin. Subsequently, through the process and power of procreation, man's sinful nature was passed down to his offspring, and mankind was incapable of paying the price to redeem himself. It would take a Righteous One to redeem fallen and corrupted man. Our dilemma is clearly revealed in the Scriptures, *"There is none righteous, no, not one"* (Rom. 3:10). But still, God told satan and us that a man would come and redeem fallen humanity. Note what God told the serpent in Eden:

And I will put enmity between thee and the woman, and between **thy seed and her seed**; *it shall bruise thy head, and thou* **shalt bruise His heel** (Genesis 3:15).

Fallen man and his corruptible body could not take himself out of the hole that he had thrown himself into. That's why God had to prepare a body, a special body for Jesus. Had He been born of natural procreation, He could have not been the Savior who would

4

redeem man, for His body would have been corruptible. His body had to be holy, sinless, and perfect. This is the reason for the virgin birth through which a Righteous One came into the earth.

Wherefore when He cometh into the world, He saith, Sacrifice and offering thou wouldest not, but a body hast Thou prepared Me (Hebrews 10:5).

*Then said Mary unto the angel, How shall this be, **seeing I know not a man?** And the angel answered and said unto her, **The Holy Ghost shall come upon thee**, and the power of the Highest shall overshadow thee: **therefore also that holy thing which shall be born** of thee shall be called the Son of God* (Luke 1:34-35).

Prior to the birth of Jesus, everyone born in the earth was born unholy and in the fallen image of Adam. The fig leaf that Adam had used to cover himself is a type of religion. God did not accept it in the Garden, and on His way to Jerusalem, Jesus cursed the fig tree and said, *"No man eat fruit of thee hereafter for ever"* (Mark 11:14). The fruit of religion can never cover or redeem man. Our hope is in the blood of Jesus—the only way for us to get to Heaven.

And being made perfect, He became the author of eternal salvation unto all them that obey Him (Hebrews 5:9).

*In this way, God qualified Him as a perfect High Priest, and He became **the source of eternal salvation** for all those who obey Him* (Hebrews 5:9 NLT).

2. *Blood is required to cover and clothe man.*

For God to clothe Adam and Eve with coats of skins or leather, an animal had to be slain and its blood shed. This brought covering to man's transgression. Fig leaves would never nor could they ever cover or atone for Adam's sin. From the Garden, God unveiled that the only suitable cover for fallen humanity is blood. For this reason, no type of angel can redeem you. Guardian angels, archangels, cherubims, and seraphims do not have blood. All through the Old Testament, the blood of millions of little lambs covered the people's sins until Jesus, the

God-Man came, and with the blood of God in His veins, He redeemed and washed man.

Who is he that overcometh the world, but he that believeth that Jesus is the Son of God? **This is He that came by water and blood, even Jesus Christ**; *not by water only, but by water and blood...* (1 John 5:5-6).

Take heed therefore unto yourselves, and to all the flock, over the which the Holy Ghost hath made you overseers, to feed the **church of God, which He hath purchased with His own blood** (Acts 20:28).

3. *The innocent will die for the guilty.*

That slain animal whose blood was shed did not do anything wrong. God showed us from the beginning that an innocent victim would pay the price for man's sin. Two thousand years ago, Jesus, the innocent, died for the guilty. We were the guilty and the unjust as we all were in Adam when he sinned. Peter in his epistle aptly penned it, *"...the just for the unjust"* (1 Pet. 3:18a). Even Judas realized this when he said, *"I have betrayed the innocent blood"* (Matt. 27:4a). God could not have provided the skin of the animal without first putting it to death and shedding its blood. God Himself provided the innocent blood sacrifice in the Garden, and He would do so again at the cross. Right there in Eden, God was saying that only He could provide the sacrifice for man. The apostle Paul echoed God's attitude when he said, *"The wages of sin is death..."* (Rom. 6:23). The consequences of sin demanded death as form of satisfactory payment. Jesus, in whom was no guilt and no sin, paid the price for us.

For Christ also hath once suffered for sins, **the just for the unjust**, *that He might bring us to God, being put to death in the flesh, but quickened by the Spirit* (1 Peter 3:18).

For Christ died for sins once and for all, **a good man on behalf of sinners**, *in order to lead you to God...* (1 Peter 3:18 Good News).

4. *A substitute will take the punishment for Adam's sin and act of high treason.*

A substitute is defined as a person or thing that takes the place or function of another. You have seen it in soccer and other team sports where a player is replaced by another, and that player's role is filled by someone else. In today's vernacular, we call it "trading places." God showed us in the Garden that a substitute would have to take the punishment. Just as that innocent animal died, Jesus became our ultimate substitute and died for all humanity. The event in Genesis was a depiction of what was to come in Jesus Christ, the perfect Lamb of God who takes away the sin of the world. Remember, God told Adam not to eat of the fruit of the tree of knowledge of good and evil. God distinctly declared, *"...for in the **day** that thou eatest thereof **thou shalt surely die**"* (Gen. 2:17, emphasis added). Notice, it clearly says death will occur on the day the fruit is partaken of. Yet we know that Adam lived after the event in the Garden and died at the age of 930. Adam did not immediately die physically; however, theologians claim that Adam died spiritually, and rightly so.

I want you to put yourself in Adam's place. He knew the decree of God, and he knew that the penalty for breaking God's decree was death. Now, imagine as he put the fruit in his mouth, chewed, and swallowed it. He may have been expecting to be zapped and killed. Yet nothing happened! Or did it? Did death occur that day? Yes, it did! Even though Adam deserved to die, he didn't; instead, God killed and shed the blood of an animal in his place. That slain animal that covered Adam was his substitute. *He saw death that day in the form of a substitute*. The innocent substitute died for the guilty. This sacrifice of an innocent animal as a substitute teaches that the penalty of sin is death, and an innocent one can die in the sinner's place therefore making atonement for him.

...For even Christ our passover is sacrificed for us (1 Corinthians 5:7).

5. *There is only one way to God—the way of the blood.*

In a world where we are being told there are many ways to God, the Bible reveals there is only one way, and that is through the blood of His Son. If a man tries any other way, Jesus said he is a thief and a robber. The only way is the blood of Jesus.

Verily, verily, I say unto you, He that entereth not by the door into the sheepfold, but climbeth up some other way, the same is a thief and a robber (John 10:1).

There are other religions that require the blood of your sons for salvation; Christianity, however, teaches us that God sent His Son and shed His blood to bring salvation to all humanity. Redemption demands that blood of a perfect substitute be shed to gain access into the presence of the Most High God. The Book of Hebrews makes an emphatic statement when it says, *"...not without blood"* (see Heb. 9:7,18). Even the Lord Jesus, our great High Priest could not enter the heavenly Holy of Holies without blood. He entered with His own sacrificial and sinless blood. The Father God accepted this offering instead of the blood of all those who were under the curse, and who were consequently polluted, helpless, and unqualified.

*And when I passed by thee, and saw thee **polluted in thine own blood**, I said unto thee when thou wast in thy blood, Live; yea, I said unto thee when thou wast in thy blood, Live (Ezekiel 16:6).*

Moses in his third book shows us the specified way to connect to God, which God revealed to him—the way of the blood. It was not something that Moses came up with as a figment of his imagination.

*The Lord called to Moses from the Tabernacle and said to him, "Give the following instructions to the Israelites: Whenever you present offerings to the Lord, you must bring animals from your flocks and herds. If your sacrifice for a whole burnt offering is from the herd, **bring a bull with no physical defects to the entrance of the Tabernacle so it will be accepted by the Lord**. Lay your hand on its head so the Lord will accept it as your substitute, thus making atonement for you. Then slaughter the animal in the Lord's presence, and Aaron's sons, the priests, will present **the blood by sprinkling** it against the sides of the altar that stands in front of the Tabernacle (Leviticus 1:1-5 NLT).*

The sacrifice had to be bloody and without any blemish or defect. God, and not man, declared the specifications. It had to be offered according to the ritual established by God.

It's All About Blood

Blood! Blood! Blood! It is all about blood. If you do not like blood, then you will not like God, your Bible, or your covenant with God. We have a blood covenant, a blood redemption, and we are blood bought. The whole Bible is about blood. It is a bloody book! Do you realize the first one to shed blood in the world was God? Contrary to traditional thinking, Cain was not the first person to shed blood; it was God. In addition, the first one in the Bible to mention blood was God.

Unto Adam also and to his wife did the Lord God make coats of skins, and clothed them (Genesis 3:21).

And He said, What hast thou done? the voice of thy brother's blood crieth unto Me from the ground (Genesis 4:10).

You must understand that blood is very sacred to God. The Books of Moses reveal three important facts about blood.

1. *God hears blood.*

And He said, What hast thou done? the voice of thy brother's blood crieth unto Me from the ground (Genesis 4:10).

The Scriptures unveil that blood has a voice. Abel's blood spoke from the ground, and God heard it. The author of the Book of Hebrews declared that the blood of Jesus speaks better things than the blood of Abel (see Heb. 12:24). The blood of Jesus has a voice, and it is speaking on your behalf. If God heard the voice of Abel's blood, then He especially hears the blood of His Son Jesus.

2. *God smells blood.*

And Noah builded an altar unto the Lord; and took of every clean beast, and of every clean fowl, and offered burnt offerings on the altar. **And the Lord smelled a sweet savour** (Genesis 8:20-21a).

Noah offered to God a blood sacrifice when he came out of the ark, and notice the expression, "...the Lord smelled a sweet savour." The sacrifice smelled good to God. Now consider what the apostle Paul reveals in his Ephesian epistle:

And walk in love, as Christ also **hath loved us, and hath given Himself for us an offering and a sacrifice to God for a sweetsmelling savour** (Ephesians 5:2).

The sacrifice of Jesus also brought a sweet aroma to the nostrils of God. *The blood of Jesus smells good to the Father all the time.*

3. *God sees blood.*

    *And the blood shall be to you for a token upon the houses where ye are: and **when I see the blood**, I will pass over you, and the plague shall not be upon you to destroy you, when I smite the land of Egypt. And this day shall be unto you for a memorial...* (Exodus 12:13-14).

    The blood was visible to God's eyes. The sight of blood over the children of Israel moved God to hover and protect them from the destroyer.

    God sees the blood of his sacrificial Lamb night and day.

    God hears blood, God smells blood, and God sees blood! When you are washed, cleansed, and covered by the blood of Jesus, God hears you when you pray! You also smell good to God. Your own cologne does not impress Him, but the blood of His Son over you is a sweet aroma to His nostrils. Furthermore, when you are covered by the blood of Jesus, God sees you. That is good news for the believer. That is good news!

Redeemed

Redeemed, how I love to proclaim it!
Redeemed by the blood of the Lamb;
Redeemed through His infinite mercy,
His child and forever I am.

*Redeemed, redeemed,
Redeemed by the blood of the Lamb;
Redeemed, redeemed,
His child and forever I am.*

Redeemed, and so happy in Jesus,
No language my rapture can tell;
I know that the light of His presence
With me doth continually dwell.

CHAPTER 2

Faith in the Blood

For whatsoever is born of God overcometh the world: and this is the victory that overcometh the world, even our faith (1 John 5:4).

Many times we have heard the expression, "Your faith overcomes the world!" As true as this statement is, untold millions of believers still continue to struggle. Some even claim, "I have faith, but I often feel defeated." So what is the problem? It seems many people do not know what the object of their faith is or how to use or release their faith in order to see results. For many, having faith in God is simply believing in the existence of God. As noble as this may sound, believing alone will not solve your problems or lead you to a life of victory. For the devil also believes in the existence of God, yet he remains defeated.

Thou believest that there is one God; thou doest well: the devils also believe, and tremble (James 2:19).

In What Should Our Faith Be?

Faith overcomes the world! But faith in what?

*Who is he that overcometh the world, but he that believeth that Jesus is the Son of God? **This is He that came by water and blood**, even Jesus Christ; not by water only, but by water and blood* (1 John 5:5-6a).

13

Notice these words—"This is He that came by water and blood, even Jesus Christ; not by water only, but by water and blood."

Here, the apostle John is trying to get your attention. Jesus Christ did not come by water only, but by water and blood. What is he talking about? Well, he is not referring to something like tap water or water baptism. In this case, water refers to the Word of God.

That He might sanctify and cleanse it with the washing of water by the word (Ephesians 5:26).

The water represents the Word. So in your mind, connect the word water with the Word. Jesus came as the Word, as John also revealed in his Gospel:

In the beginning was the Word, and the Word was with God, and the Word was God. The same was in the beginning with God. All things were made by Him; and without Him was not any thing made that was made. In Him was life; and the life was the light of men....

And the Word was made flesh, and dwelt among us... (John 1:1-4,14).

But whosoever drinketh of the water that I shall give him shall never thirst; but the water that I shall give him shall be in him a well of water springing up into everlasting life (John 4:14).

The Word was made flesh! Remember that John said that Jesus came by water (or Word) and blood. In the Old Testament, Moses declares,

For the life of the flesh is in the blood... (Leviticus 17:11).

Therefore, life is in the Word and life is in the blood. Divine life is in the Word and the blood. The body of Jesus was Word-flesh. The same Word-flesh body of Jesus carried His precious blood. Just like your body carries your blood, His body was the vessel that contained and carried His blood. The Word and the blood came together. Our faith, therefore, must be in the Word of Jesus and the blood of Jesus. In fact, according to the apostle John, every believer must have faith in the Word, blood, and spirit.

And there are three that bear witness in earth, the spirit, and the water, and the blood: and these three agree in one (1 John 5:8).

The Word, the Spirit, and the blood all agree. Having confidence in the ability of the Word, the blood of Jesus, and the Spirit of God will bring you to a place of dominion on the earth. They create in you an indomitable force that you can use to terrorize the devil. For an effective life, your confidence must be in the Word, blood, and the leading of the Holy Spirit.

> *Being justified freely by His grace through the redemption that is in Christ Jesus: whom God hath set forth to be a propitiation **through faith in His blood**, to declare His righteousness for the remission of sins that are past, through the forbearance of God* (Romans 3:24-25).

Here you see it clearly from the mouth of the apostle Paul—"faith in His blood." So the object of our faith must be the Word and the blood. Paul further enlightens us about faith in the blood:

> *Therefore **being justified by faith**, we have peace with God through our Lord Jesus Christ* (Romans 5:1).

Paul says we are justified by faith!

> *Much more then, being **now justified by His blood**, we shall be saved from wrath through Him* (Romans 5:9).

In verse 1, Paul says we are justified by faith, and in verse 9, he says the blood justifies us. So we can safely conclude that *we are justified by faith in the blood of Jesus.*

Why Should I Have Faith in the Blood of Jesus?

Even as the children of Israel had to have faith in the blood of a slain lamb during the Passover night, we also need to exercise faith in the blood of the slain Lamb of God. Following are seven reasons why you must have faith in the blood of Jesus. I call them the seven pillars of faith in the blood.

Pillar One—Sinless Blood

The virgin birth was the entrance of sinless blood in the earth. Peter, in his first Epistle, describes Jesus as the *"lamb without blemish and without spot"* (1 Pet. 1:19b). Humanity's nature, spirit, and blood had been infected by the corruption of Adam's act of high treason, but Jesus' blood was not a partaker of this corruption. Sin was transmitted through Adam, and every human being, with one exception, has been the product of Adam's sinful and corrupted seed. According to God, in Genesis 3:15, Jesus is the one exception who is known as "the seed of the woman." *Jesus did not have the virus of Adam's blood in him.*

> And **hath made of one blood all nations of men** *for to dwell on all the face of the earth, and hath determined the times before appointed, and the bounds of their habitation* (Acts 17:26).

All nations have been made from one blood—that of Adam; there-fore, all nations have corrupted blood. So, the Redeemer could not come from the seed of a man from any nation. New blood was required—pure and sinless blood. The virgin birth and the Incarnation were an absolute necessity for Jesus to be the perfect sinless blood offering. The blood in the human embryo is formed by itself. Blood does not ever pass in the embryo from the mother to child. The moth-er's blood supports the baby through the placenta thus preventing her blood from entering the baby's veins. **God is a genius!** Albert Einstein and Isaac Newton's brilliant minds pale into insignificance compared to the mind of God. I love what Paul says:

> *O the depth of the riches both of the wisdom and knowledge of God! how unsearchable are His judgments, and His ways past find-ing out! For who hath known the mind of the Lord? or who hath been His counsellor?* (Romans 11:33-34).

The body of the woman was carefully fashioned by God (see Gen. 2:22), so that in the future her womb could carry the Incarnate Man, our Redeemer, without infecting him with corrupted blood. Incarnation sim-ply means God coming in the flesh or taking human form. In our Christian context, it means the taking of bodily form by God in Jesus. Even though the word *incarnation* does not appear in the Bible, it refers to God becoming flesh.

> *In the beginning was the Word, and the Word was with God, and the Word was God....*
>
> *And the Word was made flesh, and dwelt among us, (and we beheld His glory, the glory as of the only begotten of the Father,) full of grace and truth* (John 1:1,14).

The purpose of the Incarnation was to reveal God to man and to redeem man to God.

Christ became incarnate so that He could die for the sin of humanity through the perfect sacrifice. Jesus' Father was God—not Joseph or Adam. Adam was the father of all mankind; however, Jesus was born of a virgin, and the blood that flowed in his veins was from God, resulting in *"that holy thing which shall be born of thee shall be called the Son of God"* (Luke 1:35b), with a sinless human nature. The Scriptures clearly reveal the sinlessness of Jesus; in fact, the three major writers of the New Testament testify to this fact.

Paul's Testimony

*For He hath made Him to be sin for us, **who knew no sin**; that we might be made the righteousness of God in Him* (2 Corinthians 5:21).

*For such an high priest became us, **who is holy, harmless, undefiled, separate from sinners**, and made higher than the heavens* (Hebrews 7:26).

Paul's verdict is that Jesus never sinned and had no sin in Him. He further declared that the Lord Jesus was separate from sinners in that He did not partake of the sin nature.

Peter's Testimony

*The God of Abraham, and of Isaac, and of Jacob, the God of our fathers, hath glorified His Son Jesus; whom ye delivered up, and denied Him in the presence of Pilate, when he was determined to let Him go. **But ye denied the Holy One and the Just**, and desired a murderer to be granted unto you* (Acts 3:13-14).

*For even hereunto were ye called: because Christ also suffered for us, leaving us an example, that ye should follow His steps: **who did no sin**, neither was guile found in His mouth* (1 Peter 2:21-22).

Peter's verdict is that Jesus is the Holy One and the Just. He had no sin against Him and no sin in Him.

John's Testimony

*And ye know that He was manifested to take away our sins; **and in Him is no sin*** (1 John 3:5).

John's verdict is that the Lord had no sin. All three major writers of the New Testament agree that Jesus was sinless. Even Pilate was aware that Jesus was a just, innocent, and faultless man.

> When Pilate saw that he could prevail nothing, but that rather a tumult was made, he took water, and washed his hands before the multitude, saying, I am innocent of **the blood of this just person**: see ye to it (Matthew 27:24).

> Then said Pilate to the chief priests and to the people, I find no fault in this man (Luke 23:4).

Pillar Two—Sacred Blood

Jesus' blood is the blood of the perfect man—the God Man. And because Jesus was perfect God and perfect Man, He alone, as the Lamb of God, was qualified to give His blood as ransom for sin.

> The next day John seeth Jesus coming unto him, and saith, **Behold the Lamb of God, which taketh away the sin of the world** (John 1:29).

> Forasmuch as ye know that ye were not redeemed with corruptible things, as silver and gold, from your vain conversation received by tradition from your fathers; **but with the precious blood of Christ, as of a lamb without blemish and without spot** (1 Peter 1:18-19).

The virgin birth allows us to see and understand the sacredness of the blood of Jesus. If Jesus had had an earthly father, then His blood would have been corrupted. His blood would have been that of fallen humanity. Rather, His blood was sacred because it was both divine and human. Jesus had no male parent; therefore, the life that was in His flesh was in His blood and it was literally the blood of God.

Pillar Three—Substitutionary Blood

Jesus' blood was offered and substituted in our place. A substitute is an individual who takes someone else's place. Animal sacrifices and human beings are unqualified as substitutes and cannot satisfy the demands of Heavenly Justice. Jesus is our only substitute. Consider the following Scriptures that authenticate substitution.

Who gave Himself for us, that He might redeem us from all iniquity, *and purify unto Himself a peculiar people, zealous of good works* (Titus 2:14).

*For it is **not possible** that the blood of bulls and of goats should take away sins* (Hebrews 10:4).

*How much more shall the blood of Christ, who through the eternal Spirit **offered Himself** without spot to God, purge your conscience from dead works to serve the living God?* (Hebrews 9:14).

*And that **He died for all**, that they which live should not henceforth live unto themselves...* (2 Corinthians 5:15).

*For Christ also hath once suffered for sins, **the just for the unjust**, that He might bring us to God, being put to death in the flesh, but quickened by the Spirit* (1 Peter 3:18).

*But **He was wounded** for our transgressions, **He was bruised** for our iniquities: the chastisement of our peace was upon Him; and with His stripes we are healed.*

*All we like sheep have gone astray; we have turned every one to his own way; **and the Lord hath laid on Him the iniquity of us all***

*He was oppressed, and He was afflicted, yet He opened not His mouth: **He is brought as a lamb to the slaughter, and as a sheep before her shearers is dumb, so He openeth not His mouth**.*

***He was taken from prison** and from judgment: and who shall declare His generation? for **He was cut off** out of the land of the living: for the transgression of My people was He stricken.*

And He made His grave with the wicked, and with the rich in His death; because He had done no violence, neither was any deceit in His mouth.

***Yet it pleased the Lord to bruise Him; He hath put Him to grief: when thou shalt make His soul an offering for sin**, He shall see His seed, He shall prolong His days, and the pleasure of the Lord shall prosper in His hand.*

He shall see of the travail of His soul, and shall be satisfied: by His knowledge shall My righteous servant justify many; for He shall bear their iniquities.

Therefore will I divide Him a portion with the great, and He shall divide the spoil with the strong; **because He hath poured out His soul unto death**: *and He was numbered with the transgressors;* **and He bare the sin of many, and made intercession for the transgressors** (Isaiah 53:5-12).

Although the word *substitution* is not mentioned in the Bible, it is portrayed all throughout the Scriptures. In the Old Testament, we see many pictures of substitution, which would be fulfilled by Jesus in the New Testament. Isaiah reminds us that God showed the end from the beginning. When God covered Adam and Eve after the fall, it was in the skin of an innocent animal whose blood had been shed. When Abel offered an acceptable sacrifice to God, it was that of a lamb whose blood had been shed. When Isaac was about to be sacrificed by Abraham on the mountain, it was the blood of a substitute ram that saved his life. It was said of Abraham that he would teach and *"command his children and his household after him, and they shall keep the way of the Lord, to do justice and judgment; that the Lord may bring upon Abraham that which He hath spoken of him"* (Gen. 18:19). Abraham taught both his physical and spiritual generations that their existence as a great nation is because of substitutionary blood. If there had never been substitution, Isaac would have died and the promise would have died with him. Thank God for the blood of substitution.

When the death angel was destroying Egypt, it was the sprinkled blood of a slain lamb on the door that saved God's covenant people. When Jesus died in the place of Barabbas, that was also an example of substitution. Barabbas literally means "son of the father"; Jesus, the true Son of the Father died to save humanity. *The Son of the Father gave His life so we can be reconciled to the Father of the Son.* Jesus also made references to Himself as the substitute for mankind. He said, *"I am the living bread which came down from heaven: if any man eat of this bread, he shall live for ever: and the bread that I will give is My flesh, which I will give for the life of the world"* (John 6:51). Through the Gospel of John, we see further claim made by Jesus as the substitute.

I am the good shepherd: the good shepherd giveth His life for the sheep (John 10:11).

…and I lay down My life for the sheep (John 10:15).

Over the years, millions of sheep have died as substitutes to cover the sins of the people until the perfect Lamb of God came and offered Himself as the ultimate substitute. His blood did not cover our sins but eradicated and annihilated them into the sea of forgetfulness. Following are other Scriptures that validate substitutionary blood.

...Christ died for our sins... (1 Corinthians 15:3).

...Christ died for the ungodly (Romans 5:6).

[Christ was] *made...sin for us* (2 Corinthians 5:21a).

[Christ] *bare our sins in His own body on the tree* (1 Peter 2:24a).

Christ was once offered to bear the sins of many (Hebrews 9:28a).

[Christ shed His blood] *for the remission of sins* (Romans 3:25a).

[Christ] *was wounded for our transgressions* (Isaiah 53:5a).

[Christ] *was delivered for our offenses* (Romans 4:25a).

...[Christ] *bare the sin of many...* (Isaiah 53:12).

[Christ] *gave Himself for our sins* (Galatians 1:4a).

...Christ died for us (Romans 5:8).

I am crucified with Christ: nevertheless I live; yet not I, but Christ liveth in me: and the life which I now live in the flesh I live by the faith of the Son of God, **who loved me, and gave Himself for me** (Galatians 2:20).

Pillar Four—Sacrificial Blood

One of the meanings of *sacrifice* is to bring near. The blood sacrifice of Jesus brought the sinner near to God. Jesus' blood is the blood of eternal sacrifice. God gave His Son as an eternal sacrifice. When God gave Jesus, He did not give someone whom He was happy to discard; He gave His only begotten Son. A sacrifice costs something, and it cost the Father everything to sacrifice Jesus. On the cross, Jesus willingly separated Himself from His Father so that we might be united with His Father. Today we can call God "Abba, Father" because of the sacrificial blood of the Lord.

...Christ also hath loved us, and hath given Himself for us an offering and a **sacrifice** *to God for a sweetsmelling savour* (Ephesians 5:2).

...For even Christ our passover is sacrificed for us (1 Corinthians 5:7).

Pillar Five—Sufficient Blood

*And He is the **propitiation** for our sins: and not for ours only, but also for the sins of the whole world* (1 John 2:2).

Propitiation is an unusual word that is seldom used in today's vernacular. In fact, most believers do not know what it means, yet it is very crucial for understanding our walk of faith.

Propitiation relates to an appeasing, to gain or regain the favor and goodwill of someone. Principally, it refers to the process where someone's anger or wrath is either *averted* or *satisfied*, resulting in *mercy* being received. It relates to satisfying the claims of a debtor. Classically, in pagan usage, the word *propitiation* was used to describe the averting of the wrath of the gods. The shed blood of Jesus was sufficient to satisfy God's anger against sin and brought mercy upon our lives.

For God sent Jesus to take the punishment for our sins and to satisfy God's anger against us. We are made right with God when we believe that Jesus shed His blood, sacrificing His life for us. God was being entirely fair and just when He did not punish those who sinned in former times (Romans 3:25 NLT).

According to the apostle John, Jesus is the propitiation for our sins and also for the whole world.

Herein is love, not that we loved God, but that He loved us, and sent His Son to be the propitiation for our sins (1 John 4:10).

Animal blood had no power to save or to satisfy God. It did not have the value to ransom a man's life because the animal that was killed did not bear the image of man. Whereas, according to Hebrews, Jesus' blood was offered once and for all. Never again would we have to sacrifice thousands of animals every year. Over the years, millions of little lambs have died but on Calvary's cross, the Lamb of God's blood was sufficient and satisfied the Righteous Judge of the universe. His blood was sufficient to pay the price of sin! His blood was sufficient to rent the veil that separated God from man. And His blood is sufficient to continually cleanse us from all unrighteousness. Thank God for the blood! It is the blood that satisfies!

Pillar Six—Security or Shielding Blood

The blood of Jesus is our blood of protection. John the Revelator tells us, *"...they overcame him by the blood of the Lamb"* (Rev. 12:11a). In the past, on Egypt's day of judgment, Israel was shielded from the arrows of the angel of death by the shed blood of a lamb. The blood was their defense, security, and shield against death. In addition, Paul, in his description of the armor of God, links faith to the shield. Our faith is in the blood. Faith in the blood is our shield. A Roman soldier had two different kinds of shields: One was used in combat and the other for parade—a small, round, and decorative shield (which was not the one Paul was referring to). The word *shield* in Greek is *thureos*, meaning a large oblong four-cornered shield. The root word of *thureos* is *thura* which means door. Wasn't the blood applied on the door in the Exodus? So, the shield of faith is a shield as big as a door to cover you from the top of your head to the tip of your toes. The blood of Jesus is a shield that will cover you entirely and quench all the flaming missiles of the devil. The blood-shield protects you from the past, sustains you in the present, and propels you into your future. It is safety blood.

Pillar Seven—Saving Blood

The reason we are saved today is because of the blood of Jesus. It is because of the shed blood that Jesus took into Heaven on the heavenly mercy seat that we also have access into Heaven. None of us could ever enter in without the blood.

> *Having therefore, brethren, boldness to enter into the holiest by the blood of Jesus* (Hebrews 10:19).

Not our good works, but the blood is our security of Heaven. We have been declared righteous by faith in the blood. We have peace with God by faith in the blood.

> *And, having made **peace** through the blood of His cross, by Him to reconcile all things unto Himself; by Him, I say, whether they be things in earth, or things in heaven* (Colossians 1:20).

We were enemies of God; we were aliens in God's sight. But thank God for what the blood did. The blood is our peace! The blood is our access into the grace of salvation.

Thank God for the blood!

I have faith in the blood!

Nothing But the Blood of Jesus

What can wash away my sin?
Nothing but the blood of Jesus;
What can make me whole again?
Nothing but the blood of Jesus.

Oh! precious is the flow
That makes me white as snow;
No other fount I know,
Nothing but the blood of Jesus.

For my pardon, this I see,
Nothing but the blood of Jesus;
For my cleansing this my plea,
Nothing but the blood of Jesus.

Nothing can for sin atone,
Nothing but the blood of Jesus;
Naught of good that I have done,
Nothing but the blood of Jesus.

This is all my hope and peace,
Nothing but the blood of Jesus;
This is all my righteousness,
Nothing but the blood of Jesus.

Now by this I'll overcome—
Nothing but the blood of Jesus,
Now by this I'll reach my home—
Nothing but the blood of Jesus.

Glory! Glory! This I sing—
Nothing but the blood of Jesus,
All my praise for this I bring—
Nothing but the blood of Jesus.

CHAPTER 3

The Precious Blood

> *Forasmuch as ye know that* **ye were not redeemed with corruptible things**, *as silver and gold, from your vain conversation received by tradition from your fathers; but with the* **precious blood** *of Christ, as of a lamb without blemish and without spot: who verily was foreordained before the foundation of the world, but was manifest in these last times for you* (1 Peter 1:18-20).
>
> *Christ hath redeemed us from the curse of the Law...* (Galatians 3:13).

Redemption Planned Before the Foundation of the World

First, from this point on, I want to drive into your spirit and mind the word *redeemed*. *Every time you see the words* **redeemed** *or* **redemption** *in your Bible, I want you to think of blood*, because Peter revealed you could not be redeemed without blood. Your redemption is because of blood. Your salvation is because of blood. Redemption and salvation can never be separated from the blood.

Second, notice Peter's words again: *"redeemed...with the precious blood of Christ, as of a lamb without blemish and without spot: who verily was foreordained before the foundation of the world."* The blood of Jesus was not a knee-jerk reaction from God after the sin of Adam. It is not as if God was caught surprised by satan and Adam's act of high treason. The Word reveals that the shed blood of Jesus was foreordained before the foundation of the world. The blood was a preplanned, proactive act of God to redeem mankind. John the Revelator, states that *"the Lamb* [was] *slain from the foundation of the world"* (Rev. 13:8b).

This bloodshed, in the mind of satan, however, signified death and defeat. As far as he was concerned, man was doomed. But God had a plan—a blood plan before the foundation of the world. In other words, before man ever fell, God already planned his redemption. In God's economy, the shedding of blood would mean life and victory. Had the devil known the plan and mind of God, he would have never crucified the Lord. Had he known that the shedding of Jesus' blood would have brought man in favor with God, satan would have never done what he did. Aren't you glad that God is smarter than the devil?

Precious Blood

Peter also states in his first Epistle that the blood of Jesus which redeems us is precious blood. What does that mean?

The word *precious* here does not mean cute, as when one looks at a little baby and says, "Isn't she precious?"

The word *precious* means:

- ◆ Unique and rare.
- ◆ Of great price, expensive.
- ◆ Reputable and held in honor.

Let us delve into these meanings:

Unique and Rare

The blood of Jesus is precious because it is unique, and it is unique because it is not stained with sin. It is rare blood because all the rest of humanity's blood has been contaminated with the sin and blood of Adam. And while sin and death entered the human race through the blood of Adam, divine life and peace entered the human race through the blood of Jesus.

You know the story of how Adam landed us in the dilemma we're in—first sin, then death, and no one exempt from either sin or death. That sin disturbed relations with God in everything and everyone, but the extent of the disturbance was not clear until God spelled it out in detail to Moses. So death, this huge abyss separating us from God, dominated the landscape from Adam to Moses. Even those who didn't sin precisely as Adam did by disobeying a specific command of God still had to experience this termination of life, this separation from God. **But Adam, who got us into this, also points ahead to the One who will get us out of it** (Romans 5:12-14 MSG).

Sin affected the blood of humanity. Everyone born in the earth after the fall was born in sin. Because we all physically stem from Adam, we have the same guilty blood he had.

And when I passed by thee, and saw thee polluted in thine own blood... (Ezekiel 16:6).

Only the blood of Jesus was not polluted and was without the Adamic smirch of sin. Even Judas who betrayed the Lord revealed an important truth about the blood of Jesus:

Then Judas, which had betrayed him, when he saw that he was condemned, repented himself, and brought again the thirty pieces of silver to the chief priests and elders, Saying, **I have sinned in that I have betrayed the innocent blood** (Matthew 27:3-4a).

The blood of Jesus is unique and rare because it was and is innocent blood, whereas all of us were born with guilty blood because of Adam's transgression. No sin was ever in Him. No guilt was ever in Him. And even though Judas betrayed innocent blood, and all men and women have betrayed the Innocent Blood, the blood will never betray mankind. *The blood will never betray you.*

Of Great Price, Expensive

The blood is of great value and expensive because of what it can purchase. What money could never buy, the blood has obtained.

They that trust in their wealth, and boast themselves in the multitude of their riches; **none of them can by any means redeem his brother, nor give to God a ransom for him: (for the redemption of their soul is precious,** *and it ceaseth for ever)* (Psalm 49:6-8).

29

In Romans 7:14, Paul tells us that we were "sold under sin." Adam gave us into the hands of satan and nothing could pay for our souls.

Who sold us?

Adam did!

To whom?

To the devil!

Who would buy us back and how much would it cost?

Really! **There's no such thing as self-rescue**, *pulling yourself up by your bootstraps.* **The cost of rescue is beyond our means**, *and even then it doesn't guarantee Life forever, or insurance against the Black Hole* (Psalm 49:7-9 Message Bible).

All the wealth in the world would never have been enough to meet the high demands of Justice.

In studying the dedication of Solomon's Temple, the Scriptures clearly reveal that Israel could not keep track of the amount of blood sacrifices. Remember, the sacrifices had to be without defect, and on the day of the atonement, thousands upon thousand of lambs were offered as sacrifices. The sheer number reveals the value of such a sacrifice. Yet however expensive they were, they still could not satisfy Heavenly Justice. Likewise, there is no amount that you and I could ever pay to deliver ourselves. The world with all its glory and wonders cannot be exchanged for the redemption of mankind. A invaluable ransom was needed and there was nothing we could do or possess to redeem ourselves. Only the blood of Jesus could meet and legally satisfy the Supreme Court and the demands of satan. His blood was sufficient for all of mankind. His blood has value.

The redemption of the soul is precious and it took the precious blood to redeem a precious soul.

Take heed therefore unto yourselves, and to all the flock, over the which the Holy Ghost hath made you overseers, to feed the church of God, which He hath purchased with His own blood (Acts 20:28).

Not only is the blood valuable because of what it can purchase, but it is also costly because of what it isn't.

The blood of Jesus is of great value because the blood is not corruptible.

To be corruptible means:

◆ Become contaminated or tainted by something else.

◆ Putrid and decomposing.

◆ Containing undesirable changes in meaning.

◆ Errors made in copying.

The blood of Jesus is not contaminated or tainted. It is not putrid, decomposing, or decaying. The blood cannot be copied and does not change in content. It is still fresh today.

Reputable and Held in Honor

The blood has an unconquerable reputation because of what it has achieved and continues to achieve today.

The blood paid the demands for mankind.

The blood broke and overcame the power of satan.

The blood stopped the destroyer.

The blood broke the curse and power of sin.

The blood brings peace.

The blood cleanses today as it did 2,000 years ago.

In Heaven they sing about the blood.

On earth we sing about the blood.

In hell they fear the blood.

Three Witnesses

Peter, in his two Epistles, unveils three precious truths.

The Blood Is Precious

*Forasmuch as ye know that ye were not redeemed with corruptible things, as silver and gold, from your vain conversation received by tradition from your fathers; but with the **precious blood** of Christ, as of a lamb without blemish and without spot* (1 Peter 1:18-19).

Faith Is Precious

*Simon Peter, a servant and an apostle of Jesus Christ, to them that have obtained like **precious faith** with us through the righteousness of God and our Saviour Jesus Christ (2 Peter 1:1).*

God's Promises Are Precious

*Whereby are given unto us exceeding great and **precious promises**: that by these ye might be partakers of the divine nature, having escaped the corruption that is in the world through lust (2 Peter 1:4).*

Remember, *precious* means costly and highly esteemed. What a privilege to have at our disposal precious faith, precious blood, and precious promises. I have faith in the blood and the promises of God to deliver me.

There Is a Fountain Filled With Blood

There is a fountain filled with blood
drawn from Emmanuel's veins;
And sinners plunged beneath that
flood lose all their guilty stains.
Lose all their guilty stains,
lose all their guilty stains;
And sinners plunged beneath that
flood lose all their guilty stains.

The dying thief rejoiced to see
that fountain in his day;
And there have I, though vile as
he, washed all my sins away.
Washed all my sins away, washed
all my sins away;
And there have I, though vile as he,
washed all my sins away.

Dear dying Lamb, Thy precious
blood shall never lose its power
Till all the ransomed Church of God
be saved, to sin no more.
Be saved, to sin no more, be saved,
to sin no more;
Till all the ransomed Church of
God be saved, to sin no more.

E'er since, by faith, I saw the stream
Thy flowing wounds supply,
Redeeming love has been my
theme, and shall be till I die.
And shall be till I die,
and shall be till I die;
Redeeming love has been my
theme, and shall be till I die.

Then in a nobler, sweeter song,
I'll sing Thy power to save,
When this poor lisping, stammering
tongue lies silent in the grave.
Lies silent in the grave,
lies silent in the grave;
When this poor lisping, stammering
tongue lies silent in the grave.

Lord, I believe Thou hast prepared,
unworthy though I be,
For me a blood-bought free
reward, a golden harp for me!
'Tis strung and tuned for endless
years, and formed by power divine,
To sound in God the Father's
ears no other name but Thine.

CHAPTER 4

The Benefits of the Blood

Thus far we have discovered that blood is sacred to God. He sees blood, smells blood, and hears blood. We also understand that the blood of Jesus is an effective weapon against the powers of darkness and that satan has no defense against the blood. The blood is his eternal downfall and his loss of grip on humanity.

Now we want to look at the many benefits of the blood of Jesus. These benefits are not placed in any particular order of importance, for they all are equally significant and necessary for the believer's well-being. May you enjoy meditating on the benefits that the blood of Jesus provides for you today.

A) Redemption

In whom we have redemption through His blood, the forgiveness of sins, according to the riches of His grace (Ephesians 1:7).

Redemption means:

- ◆ A releasing effected by payment of ransom.
- ◆ Deliverance.
- ◆ Liberation procured by the payment of a ransom.
- ◆ Out of the marketplace.

Redemption implies that a ransom price has been paid, and the Old Testament policy of redemption, likewise, conveys the thought of liberation by payment of a ransom price. The redemption could be that of a person, property, or an inheritance. If a person fell into serious debt, and even after liquidating his assets still could not pay the claims of his creditors, he would then mortgage himself, his life, and his family—as in the case of the widow who came to Elisha for help after the creditor came to take her two sons as slaves, as a form of payment for her husband's debt.

Let us examine what God says about redemption:

*If a resident foreigner becomes rich, and if some of your Israelite relatives go bankrupt and sell themselves to such a foreigner, they still retain the right of redemption. They may be bought back **by a close relative—an uncle, a nephew, or anyone else who is closely related**. They may also redeem themselves if they can get the money* (Leviticus 25:47-49 NLT).

After that he is sold he may be redeemed again; one of his brethren may redeem him (Leviticus 25:48).

We know that as sinners we cannot redeem ourselves, for Adam sold us without having the means of redemption. But notice in the Scriptures above that redemption can be procured by a close relative or a next of kin, and this is where we get the term *kinsman-redeemer*. A prime example can be seen in the lives of Ruth and Boaz.

And I thought to advertise thee, saying, Buy it before the inhabitants, and before the elders of my people. If thou wilt redeem it, redeem it: but if thou wilt not redeem it, then tell me, that I may know: for there is none to redeem it beside thee; and I am after thee. And he said, I will redeem it.

Then said Boaz, What day thou buyest the field of the hand of Naomi, thou must buy it also of Ruth the Moabitess, the wife of the dead, to raise up the name of the dead upon his inheritance.

And the kinsman said, I cannot redeem it for myself, lest I mar mine own inheritance: redeem thou my right to thyself; for I cannot redeem it.

Now this was the manner in former time in Israel concerning redeeming and concerning changing, for to confirm all things; a man plucked off his shoe, and gave it to his neighbour: and this was a testimony in Israel (Ruth 4:4-7).

Boaz became Ruth's kinsman-redeemer, giving us a perfect picture of what Jesus as our Kinsman-Redeemer would do for us when He came down to earth.

Because God's children are human beings—made of flesh and blood—Jesus also became flesh and blood by being born in human form. For only as a human being could He die, and only by dying could He break the power of the devil, who had the power of death.

Only in this way could He deliver those who have lived all their lives as slaves to the fear of dying. We all know that Jesus came to help the descendants of Abraham, not to help the angels.

Therefore, it was necessary for Jesus to be in every respect like us, His brothers and sisters, so that He could be our merciful and faithful High Priest before God... (Hebrews 2:14-17 NLT).

The Kinsman-Redeemer had to pay the full price for a legal redemption, and Jesus did so with His own divine blood. Paul reminded the church in Corinth that we were bought with a price, and Peter emphasized that the payment was the precious blood of Jesus.

In studying the New Testament, there are four Greek words used to translate the word *redemption*. It is imperative for you to understand each of these words.

a) *Agorazo*: to purchase in the market.

b) *Exagorazo*: to purchase out of the market.

c) *Lutroo*: to loosen and set free.

d) *Apolutrosis*: to return to original status through the paying of ransom.

These four words clearly describe what Jesus had to do in order to redeem and deliver us. I want you to pay very close attention to the words, "out of the marketplace." Paul paints a picture of the sinner as a slave in the slave market. When Adam and Eve sinned, they voluntarily walked into the slave market. Although God had created them in His image as free moral agents, through sin they sold themselves and their generations to a life of bondage to satan, sin, and death.

And God said, **Let Us make man in Our image**, *after Our likeness: and let them have dominion over the fish of the sea, and over the fowl of the air, and over the cattle, and over all the earth, and over every creeping thing that creepeth upon the earth.* **So God created man in His own image**, *in the image of God created He him; male and female created He them* (Genesis 1:26-27).

Here is an important point to remember:

God created Adam and Eve in His image, meaning they were free, with dominion, and in power. After they sinned, however, all their descendants were born in the earth after the image and likeness of fallen Adam and Eve. Because they had become fallen slaves to satan, all their generations were thereafter born in slavery. The law of Genesis states that everything reproduces after its kind. Slaves can give birth only to slaves, and only a free man can liberate and bring deliverance to a slave.

Since creation, there have been only three persons who have come to earth free. Adam and Eve were first created free, and Jesus Christ was born free. Once again, we see the necessity and value of the virgin birth. Only Jesus was qualified to pay the ransom with His blood and liberate us from the slave market and the wicked taskmaster. The Book of Hebrews states, *"Forasmuch then as the children are partakers of flesh and blood, He also Himself likewise took part of the same..."* (Heb. 2:14), and through His shed blood, He paid the ransom-price for our redemption.

In olden days, slave markets were very common. Potential buyers would go to the market to bid for and buy slaves. But even when the slaves were purchased by another owner, their slave status did not change. They were still slaves, although they had a different master or owner. They could be sold again and again. Even though a price was paid for a slave, he was still not free; he simply went to a different location of bondage and hardship. The Lord, however, did not just buy us from satan so that we would become enslaved to another taskmaster. Jesus paid the price with His blood to take us away from the marketplace forever, never to go there again.

Even as the Son of man came not to be ministered unto, but to minister, and to give His life a ransom for many (Matthew 20:28).

Having done so, He changed our identity and status. We became new creatures in Christ Jesus. Our past has been done away with as if it never existed. Just as Meshach, Shadrach, and Abednego had no smell of smoke on them after they came out of the burning fiery furnace, the same applies to you and I. Through the cleansing power of the blood, we no longer have the former aroma of sin on us. Today, because of Jesus, we are no longer children of wickedness, for He has taken us out of the slave market to become sons and daughters of God. Through the redemption of blood, we have been delivered from the kingdom and authority of darkness.

Redemption also means change of ownership and proprietor. You must realize you no longer belong to the devil but now you belong to God.

> *For **ye are bought with a price**: therefore glorify God in **your body, and in your spirit, which are God's*** (1 Corinthians 6:20).

> *...Thou wast slain, and hast redeemed us **to God** by thy blood...* (Revelation 5:9).

Notice that we are redeemed "to God." Because of this fact, He has re-created our spirit man, and in the near future our bodies will also be redeemed from corruption to incorruption. What a day that will be! Thank God we belong to Him. We emphatically echo what Paul said of himself in many of his letters—"a slave of Jesus Christ." We are children of God by nature, but His slaves by choice.

B) New Covenant Relationship

Our covenant with God is on the basis of the shed blood of Jesus. The word *covenant* in the Scriptures is the Hebrew word *berith* meaning "to cut" or "where blood flows." It is more accurately defined as "to cut until bleeding occurs or blood flows." Hence, every time you see the word *covenant*, you should think "the flow of blood." When the Bible says, "We have a better covenant with better promises", this can be easily translated to "We have a better flow of blood with better promises." The sign of the old covenant was circumcision, along with the shed blood of sacrificial animals. In the new covenant, Christ became the sacrificial Lamb and shed blood for us.

> *Wherefore remember, that ye being in time past Gentiles in the flesh, who are called Uncircumcision by that which is called the*

Circumcision in the flesh made by hands; that at that time ye were without Christ, being aliens from the commonwealth of Israel, and strangers from the covenants of promise, having no hope, and without God in the world: but now in Christ Jesus ye who sometimes were far off are made nigh by the blood of Christ (Ephesians 2:11-13).

A covenant is more than just an agreement; it is a connection with the Most High God. Our access to a covenant relationship with God can be a reality only because of Jesus' shed blood. According to the apostle Paul in his Ephesians' Epistle, without the blood we were:

Without Christ, which means to be without the anointing.

- Aliens from the commonwealth of Israel.
- Strangers from the covenants of promise.
- Without hope.
- Without God in the world.
- Far off.

What a terrible position to be in! Thank God, Paul did not stop there.

Now *therefore ye are* **no more** *strangers and foreigners, but fellowcitizens with the saints, and of the household of God* (Ephesians 2:19).

I want you to pay attention to these two words—"no more." Whatever I used to be, now is no more a reality.

- *I used to be Christless without the anointing, but now no more.*
- *I used to be an alien, but now no more.*
- *I used to be a stranger but now no more.*
- *I used to be without hope, but now no more.*
- *I used to be without God in the world, but now no more.*
- *I used to be far off, but now no more.*
- *I used to be defeated, but now no more.*
- *I used to be fearful, but now no more.*
- *I used to be depressed, but now no more.*

- *I used to be sick, but now no more.*

- *I used to be cursed, but now no more.*

- *I used to be overlooked, but now no more.*

- *I used to be denied, but now no more.*

- *I used to be overwhelmed, but now no more.*

- *I used to be broke, but now no more.*

*Now when I passed by thee, and looked upon thee, behold, thy time was the time of love; and I spread My skirt over thee, and covered thy nakedness: yea, I sware unto thee, **and entered into a covenant with thee, saith the Lord God, and thou becamest Mine**. Then washed I thee with water; yea, I thoroughly washed away thy blood from thee, and I anointed thee with oil* (Ezekiel 16:8-9).

...there is a friend that sticketh closer than a brother (Proverbs 18:24).

Today we are God's covenant friend because of the blood of Jesus. The blood was the mercy of God in action to renew a relationship that was lost by Adam. God said through the prophet Ezekiel, "Thou becamest Mine." We belong to God because of the blood covenant.

C) Propitiation

The word *propitiation* appears only three times in the Authorized Version. The apostle John uses it twice in his first Epistle, and Paul once in the Book of Romans. *Propitiation*, an unusual word, is very important for our victory walk of faith.

*Whom God hath set forth to be a **propitiation** through faith in His blood, to declare His righteousness for the remission of sins that are past, through the forbearance of God* (Romans 3:25).

For God sent Jesus to take the punishment for our sins and to satisfy God's anger against us. We are made right with God when we believe that Jesus shed His blood, sacrificing His life for us. God was being entirely fair and just when He did not punish those who sinned in former times (Romans 3:25 NLT).

*My little children, these things write I unto you, that ye sin not. And if any man sin, we have an advocate with the Father, Jesus Christ the righteous: and He is the **propitiation** for our sins: and not for ours only, but also for the sins of the whole world* (1 John 2:1-2).

*Herein is love, not that we loved God, but that He loved us, and sent His Son to be the **propitiation** for our sins* (1 John 4:10).

Propitiation means:

◆ Relating to an appeasing or expiating (taking sin away).

◆ Having placating or expiating force, expiatory.

◆ A means of appeasing or expiating and satisfying.

The Greek word for propitiation is *hilasmos,* meaning "merciful, propitious." This reveals "a recompense, a means by which sin is covered and paid for." Principally, it refers to the process where someone's anger or wrath is either *averted* or *satisfied,* resulting in *mercy* being received. Pagans used the word to describe averting the wrath of the gods. As I previously mentioned, propitiation deals with satisfying the claims of a debtor. Twice in his Epistle, the apostle John mentions the Lord Jesus as "the propitiation," revealing that through His sacrifice of Himself, God gives mercy to the sinner who believes on Christ. Through the shed blood of Jesus, the wrath of God was averted from us. His blood satisfied God's anger against sin, met the demands of justice, and brought mercy over our lives. Thank God for the blood! It is our Mercy Seat.

God sacrificed Jesus on the altar of the world to clear that world of sin. Having faith in Him sets us in the clear. God decided on this course of action in full view of the public—to set the world in the clear with Himself through the sacrifice of Jesus, finally taking care of the sins He had so patiently endured (Romans 3:25 MSG).

D) Justification

Justification means:

◆ To be absolved from all sins.

◆ To be declared righteous.

Therefore being justified by faith, we have peace with God through our Lord Jesus Christ....Much more then, being now justified by His blood, we shall be saved from wrath through Him (Romans 5:1,9).

Because of the shed blood of Jesus, we are declared righteous and made righteous. Through the blood, we are presented holy, unblamable, and unreprovable in God's sight. To be righteous means that you possess the ability to stand before a holy God without the sense of failure and sin. Righteousness gives you a winning consciousness. You did not justify yourself, but Jesus' blood justified you. By the vicarious death of Jesus Christ, you are declared righteous and made righteous. To be justified means *just as if* you had never sinned. What a thought! The slate has been wiped clean. The blood of Jesus did not cover your sins but obliterated your sins. To be justified also means to be set right and be fit for God. The precious blood of Jesus has made you right and you are fit to be in God's presence.

*By entering through faith into what God has always wanted to do for us—***set us right with Him—make us fit for Him***—we have it all together with God because of our Master Jesus....*

Now that we are set right with God by means of this sacrificial death, **the consummate blood sacrifice***, there is no longer a question of being at odds with God in any way* (Romans 5:1,9 MSG).

E) Remission

Remission means:

- ◆ The washing away of sins.
- ◆ The cleansing of sins.
- ◆ The taking away of sins.
- ◆ Release from bondage or imprisonment, letting our sins go as if they had never been committed.

If our sins are remitted, they no longer exist; and in the absence of our sins, we are now free, cleansed, and delivered.

And almost all things are by the law purged with blood; and without shedding of blood is no remission (Hebrews 9:22).

F) Reconciliation

Reconciliation means:

- To change, exchange, as with coins for others of equivalent value.
- To reconcile (those who are at variance).
- Return to favor with.
- To receive one into favor.
- Harmonious relationship or that which brings about such a relationship.

We were enemies of God and were called aliens, but Jesus died in our stead in order to reconcile us to God. *"And, having made peace through the blood of His cross, by Him to reconcile all things unto Himself; by Him, I say, whether they be things in earth, or things in heaven"* (Col. 1:20). I especially like the fact that *reconcile* means to be back in favor with. The blood of Jesus is the blood of favor with God. It is the blood of preferential treatment. Allow me to share a story.

London to Chicago

When I first started travelling extensively, I knew nothing about mileage accumulation and very little about travelling first class. In fact, I thought travelling first class was only for people who had lots of money, and I continued to travel tourist class until somebody informed me about mileage accumulation.

One day as I was travelling from London to Chicago, I went to check in as usual, when an agent looked at me and said, "Sir, the plane is full in tourist class. Would you mind if you were upgraded to first class?"

I answered, "Would I mind? No, I don't mind at all!"

If anyone deserves upgrading, it is me. I am a child of God. And anyone who is a child of the King already has first-class status.

Once on the plane, I was shocked to discover the differences between first class and tourist class. In first class, you are offered a choice of juice or champagne. In tourist class, you receive a glass of water. In tourist class, when you fall asleep, they leave you alone in your small, uncomfortable seat. In first class, they constantly see to your need and comfort in your plush seat.

"Sir, do you want filet mignon?"

"Well, bring it on."

"Sir, do you want ice cream?"

"Do I want ice cream? I *am* Mr. Ice cream. Bring it on!"

"Sir, would you like some chocolate?"

"Bring it on."

Whatever they offered, I accepted and enjoyed; and I started praying, "Lord, don't let this plane land." I was really enjoying the preferential treatment in the favorable position that I was in. Likewise, when you are covered by the blood of Jesus, you will enjoy the preferential treatment that it provides. The blood of Jesus will treat you better than anything else on earth. The apostle Paul echoed this truth two millennia ago:

> ...*If God be for us, who can be against us?* **He that spared not His own Son, but delivered Him up for us all, how shall He not with Him also freely give us all things?** (Romans 8:31-32).

The blood that brought you back in favor with God is the same force that will release further preferential treatment in all areas of your life. The blood is your access to favor in heaven and on earth. When the favor of God is in your life, your enemies will be helpless and frustrated.

From today favor will encompass your life because of the blood. This is your time of favor.

> *Thou shalt arise, and have mercy upon Zion: for the time to favour her, yea, the set time, is come* (Psalm 102;13).

What time is it? It's favor time! Because of the blood of favor you will be:

- *Supernaturally increased and promoted.*
- *Triumphing over your enemies.*
- *Blessed coming in and blessed going out.*
- *Victorious over demons and circumstances.*
- *Receiving help from unexpected sources.*

◆ *Laughing and rejoicing.*

Confession: Because of the blood of Jesus, I expect favor to be in my life wherever I go and whatever I do. From now on, I see myself blessed!

G) Sanctification

Sanctification means:

1. To make something holy.
2. To free somebody from sin.
3. To set apart.

The death of Jesus and the blood shed serves to set apart the believer to function in holiness, as God intended. *"Jesus...that He might sanctify the people with His own blood, suffered* [outside] *the gate"* (Heb. 13:12). Jesus went to the cross so that you and I might become holy. He shed His own blood so that our lives may become clean. Holiness has a twofold meaning: First, it means "set apart for God" or "separate unto God." The blood of Jesus Christ sets us apart marking us as God's property. Second, holiness means "to be pure and without sin" or "separate from the world." The blood of Jesus Christ cleanses us from sin and helps us to walk a life of purity today. We cannot achieve any degree of holiness by our own fleshly works. We succeed in holiness only through the blood.

H) Forgiveness

According to Strong's Exhaustive Concordance, forgiveness means:

◆ Release from bondage or imprisonment.

◆ Pardon of sins (letting them go as if they had never been committed).

What a powerful explanation! Released, as if sins have never been committed. The slate is wiped clean.

In whom we have redemption through His blood, the forgiveness of sins, according to the riches of His grace (Ephesians 1:7).

And according to the Law, one may almost say, all things are cleansed with blood, and without shedding of blood there is no forgiveness (Hebrews 9:22 NAS).

In the Old Testament, the blood of bulls and goats could only cover sin. That was called "atonement." But the blood of Jesus obliterates your sin so that it can never be seen again. Consequently, you stand righteous before God as if you had never sinned.

I) Peace With God

*And, having made **peace** through the blood of His cross, by Him to reconcile all things unto Himself; by Him, I say, whether they be things in earth, or things in heaven* (Colossians 1:20).

The Bible reveals to us that there are two kinds of peace.

Peace with God—justifying peace—believer's standing.

Peace of God—sanctifying peace—believer's state.

One type of peace refers to your standing, and the other to your state or condition. The differences between standing and state are as follows:

Believer's Standing

1. The believer's standing or peace *with* God is the result of the work of Jesus at Calvary. It has nothing to do with what I did or will do. I cannot add to it or take away from it.

2. I receive it the moment I am saved. It is due to the grace of God.

3. It is a done deal. I cannot improve on it or make it better by good works. It is already the best it will ever be.

4. Every believer has the same standing, same equal position, and same equal status.

Believer's State

The believer's state has to do with the actual present spiritual condition or state he is in. It has to do with the believer's walk and actions, and whether he chooses to be a doer of the Word. His state will depend upon many factors, such as whether he trusts God or not, whether he remains in Christ or not, whether he obeys the Word of God or not.

Peace with God refers to our being reconciled to God by the shed blood of Jesus. We are no longer aliens and enemies of God, but stand as a chosen generation and a royal priesthood.

*Therefore being **justified** by faith, we have **peace with God through our Lord Jesus Christ: by whom also we have access** by faith into this grace wherein we stand, and rejoice in hope of the glory of God* (Romans 5:1-2).

"Peace with God" refers to our justification imparted to us by Jesus. That is why it is called justifying peace. Every person who has received Jesus as his or her Lord and Savior has that peace. It is our access to God and His access to us. Justification has to do with your spirit man being made a new creature in Christ Jesus.

"Peace of God" refers to the believer's mind being tranquil and free from worry. It is available to all, but unfortunately, not every believer enjoys that kind of peace. This kind of peace comes from acting on the Word.

Be careful for nothing; *but in every thing by prayer and supplication with thanksgiving let your requests be made known unto God.* **And the peace of God**, *which passeth all understanding, shall keep your hearts and minds through Christ Jesus* (Philippians 4:6-8).

"Be careful for nothing" simply means, don't worry about anything.

"Well, Brother Glenn, everybody worries." No! Only those who do not know the Word worry.

"Well, what am I supposed to do with all my worries then?"

Do what the Bible says, and cast them all upon Jesus (see 1 Pet. 5:7).

The blood of Jesus is the blood of reconciliation. It is the blood that has brought God and us together. Now we have peace with God.

J) *Purges the Consciousness*

Through the one sacrifice of Jesus, the consciousness of sin has been removed. Whereas, in the Old Testament, people were required to sacrifice every year, a constant reminder that they were sinners, now, through the blood of Jesus, our conscience is cleansed.

"The blood of Christ…purge[s] your conscience from dead works to serve the living God" (Heb. 9:14b). *"The blood of Jesus Christ His Son cleanseth us from all sin"* (1 John 1:7b). There is no force on earth that can cleanse the conscience of a man. Many people may try to dull their conscience by constantly ignoring their own wrongdoings or sins, but

the guilt is still lurking within the recesses of their mind waiting to pounce at any moment. Only the blood of Jesus can truly deliver a man from guilt and inferiority complex.

K) Access to God

Access means:

◆ The right and opportunity to meet somebody.

◆ To have the opportunity or right to experience or make use of something.

There can be no access to God and the heavenly things unless our sins that separate us from Him are dealt with in death. Our access of opportunity with God is through the blood of Jesus. According to the apostle Paul, the Gentiles were brought near to God *"by the blood of Christ"* (Eph. 2:13b). A believer has total confidence and access to enter the Holy Place by the blood of Jesus.

Having therefore, brethren, boldness to enter into the holiest by the blood of Jesus, by a new and living way, which He hath consecrated for us, through the veil, that is to say, His flesh (Hebrews 10:19-20).

Through the blood of Jesus, you can enter into the very presence of God and into your land flowing with milk and honey. I particularly like the meaning of access, "to have the opportunity or right to experience or make use of something." Because of the blood, you have a divine right to experience certain things that were purchased. It is not only for a few privileged ones, but free for all. The blood gives you the right of access.

*Therefore being justified by faith, we have peace with God through our Lord Jesus Christ: by whom also we have **access by faith** into this grace wherein we stand...* (Romans 5:1-2).

In whom we have boldness and access with confidence by the faith of Him (Ephesians 3:12).

Let us therefore come boldly unto the throne of grace, that we may obtain mercy, and find grace to help in time of need (Hebrews 4:16).

*Having therefore, brethren, **boldness to enter into the holiest by the blood of Jesus**...*(Hebrews 10:19).

Our access to the throne is through the blood of Jesus. The blood of Jesus is also our access to help in time of need. When you need help, you need the blood.

The blood is:

♦ Your access to the favor of God.

♦ Your access to your redemption inheritance.

♦ Your access to the authority of the name of Jesus.

♦ Your access to divine blessing.

♦ Your access to the more abundant life.

♦ Your access to help in time of need.

L) Dominion Over Evil

A believer indwelt by the Spirit of God is an overcomer because of the blood. I want you to understand that although satan hates the blood, he has no weapon in his arsenal against the blood of Jesus.

> *Forasmuch then as the children are partakers of flesh and blood, He also Himself likewise took part of the same; that through death He might destroy him that had the power of death, that is, the devil* (Hebrews 2:14).

> *And they overcame him by the blood of the Lamb, and by the word of their testimony; and they loved not their lives unto the death* (Revelation 12:11).

You need to remember that the destroyer could not touch and harm those who had applied the blood upon the doors in Egypt. Even though the blood was just the blood of an animal, the destroyer still could not touch them. How much more powerful then is the blood of the spotless Son of God? Satan and all his cohorts are no match for the blood of Jesus.

In this Bible story, do not, for one moment, think that God was the destroyer. Many have incorrectly determined that when God said, "When I see the blood, I will pass over you," that God Himself was the destroyer and that He killed all the firstborn of Egypt. That is not a true picture of God. He is not the destroyer!

Then who was the destroyer?

*For the Lord will pass through to smite the Egyptians; and when He seeth the blood upon the lintel, and on the two side posts, the Lord will pass over the door, and **will not suffer the destroyer** to come in unto your houses to smite you* (Exodus 12:23).

Notice that God would stop the destroyer from entering their houses. Clearly, God is not the destroyer. This term is a name connected to the devil.

And they had a king over them, which is the angel of the bottomless pit, whose name in the Hebrew tongue is Abaddon, but in the Greek tongue hath his name Apollyon (Revelation 9:11).

Both Abaddon and Apollyon mean "the destroyer" in their respective languages. This name was given to satan, the angel-prince of the infernal regions, the minister of death, and the author of havoc on the earth (see Strong's Concordance). Yet he was stopped by the blood. The application of the blood on the door rendered the destroyer helpless and ineffective. The blood frustrated his plans. It will do the same for you! Through the blood of Jesus, you can frustrate satan out of your life.

"I Love Chicken"

I was 23 years old when I first travelled to Africa to minister, but before I embarked on this trip, I received all kind of information from well-meaning people. Unfortunately, much of their supposedly good advice turned out be based on fear.

"Take this with you…."

"Don't drink the water!"

"Don't eat the chicken!"

I thought about that! Don't eat chicken. What's the point of that? I love chicken! So I asked, "Well, why not?"

"Well, where you are going, they worship a spirit called mamiwater, and they sacrifice chicken to it."

Now, I do not know all the facts concerning any spirits, but one thing I do know, they all must bow before the name and blood of Jesus.

51

I simply said, "I don't know mamiwater, but I tell you what—bring on mamiwater, daddywater, and babywater (if they exist). I'm not worried about them."

When I arrived in Africa, I was asked what I wanted to eat, and you guessed it...I said, "Give me chicken!" I figured no matter how many chicken they killed and no matter how much blood was shed, it would still be no match to the blood of Jesus. I ate chicken, and I'm still here to tell you about the blood of Jesus. There is power over witchcraft and sorcery through the blood of Jesus.

I continue to travel all around the world in an age of terrorism, fear, and uncertainty; and as surely as I know my name, I know I have dominion by the blood of Jesus to reverse any plan of satan against me. I thank God for the precious blood.

M) Protection and Blessings

> ...If God be for us, who can be against us? He that spared not His own Son, but delivered Him up for us all, how shall He not with Him also freely give us all things?...For I am persuaded, that neither death, nor life, nor angels, nor principalities, nor powers, nor things present, nor things to come, nor height, nor depth, nor any other creature, shall be able to separate us from the love of God, which is in Christ Jesus our Lord (Romans 8:31-32,38-39).

If God was willing to shed the blood of His own Son to save you, then all other blessings are lightweight in comparison. It is very important to pour this into your spirit! Paul emphasized that Jesus' blood was shed for your redemption and consequently all other blessings would flow freely in your life too. There are blessings in the blood—there is a house for you in the blood; there is a car in the blood; everything you need and will ever need is in the blood.

There is also protection in the blood. In the Old Testament, we read about the Egyptians who had no protection from the destroyer, whereas the people of Israel who smeared the blood of a lamb on their houses were safe. The destroyer was refused entrance to the Hebrews' homes. Likewise, you can ensure that the destroyer remains outside your home! Everything that happened in the Old Testament is a picture and a shadow of what belongs to us in the New Testament.

Then Moses called for all the elders of Israel, and said unto them, Draw out and take you a lamb according to your families, and kill the passover.

And ye shall take a bunch of hyssop, and dip it in the blood that is in the basin, and strike the lintel and the two side posts with the blood that is in the basin; and none of you shall go out at the door of his house until the morning.

For the Lord will pass through to smite the Egyptians; and when He seeth the blood upon the lintel, and on the two side posts, the Lord will pass over the door, and will not suffer the destroyer to come in unto your houses to smite you.

And ye shall observe this thing for an ordinance to thee and to thy sons for ever (Exodus 12:21-24).

Think not that I am come to destroy the law, or the prophets: **I am not come to destroy, but to fulfil** (Matthew 5:17).

"The law and the prophets" refer to the Scriptures, and Jesus came to fulfill the Scriptures. Just as God protected the Old Testament saints by the blood, He will also protect His people today. He is a God who does not change.

You can keep the devil out of your house, you can keep him him out of your body, and you can keep him off your premises by the blood of Jesus. I love what God says He will do when He sees the blood:

And the blood shall be to you for a token upon the houses where ye are: and when I see the blood, I will pass over you, and the plague shall not be upon you to destroy you... (Exodus 12:13).

"When I see the blood, I will pass over you." The word passover literally means, "to watch over" and "to hover on and sit upon." I love that! God said when He saw the blood, He would watch over, hover on, and sit upon Israel so that the destroyer could not harm them. When the blood covers you, God will watch over, hover on, and sit upon you so that no weapon formed against you can prosper. The blood is the blood of protection, which is also evident in the life of Rahab the prostitute, famous for her scarlet thread.

Now therefore, I pray you, swear unto me by the Lord, since I have shown you kindness, that ye will also show kindness unto my father's house, and give me a true token: **and that ye will save alive my father, and my mother, and my brethren, and my sisters, and all that they have, and deliver our lives from death.**

And the men answered her, Our life for yours, if ye utter not this our business. And it shall be, when the Lord hath given us the land, that we will deal kindly and truly with thee.

Then she let them down by a cord through the window: for her house was upon the town wall, and she dwelt upon the wall.

And she said unto them, Get you to the mountain, lest the pursuers meet you; and hide yourselves there three days, until the pursuers be returned: and afterward may ye go your way.

And the men said unto her, We will be blameless of this thine oath which thou hast made us swear.

Behold, when we come into the land, thou shalt bind this line of scarlet thread in the window which thou didst let us down by: and thou shalt bring thy father, and thy mother, and thy brethren, and all thy father's household, home unto thee.

And it shall be, that whosoever shall go out of the doors of thy house into the street, his blood shall be upon his head, and we will be guiltless: and whosoever shall be with thee in the house, his blood shall be on our head, if any hand be upon him.

And if thou utter this our business, then we will be quit of thine oath which thou hast made us to swear.

And she said, **According unto your words, so be it. And she sent them away, and they departed: and she bound the scarlet line in the window** (Joshua 2:12-21).

And the city shall be accursed, even it, and all that are therein, to the Lord: only Rahab the harlot shall live, she and all that are with her in the house, because she hid the messengers that we sent....

And Joshua saved Rahab the harlot alive, and her father's house-hold, **and all that she had**; *and she dwelleth in Israel even unto this day; because she hid the messengers, which Joshua sent to spy out Jericho* (Joshua 6:17,25).

We can clearly see that the *scarlet thread,* a type of the blood of Jesus, protected not only Rahab and her family, but all of her belongings as well. God can both save your life and your possessions! You need only to learn to draw a bloodline over you and your house so that satan has no right and power to trespass.

By faith the harlot Rahab perished not with them that believed not, when she had received the spies with peace (Hebrews 11:31).

By an act of faith, Rahab, the Jericho harlot, welcomed the spies and **escaped the destruction** *that came on those who refused to trust God* (Hebrews 11:31 MSG).

Flight Back to Lagos

During one of my many mission trips to Nigeria, I had been ministering in the city of Port Harcourt during a weekend and was heading back to Lagos the following Monday morning on BellView Airline. Everything seemed to be going fine. The weather was good, we were on time, and all looked well in the natural. However, I did have a feeling in my spirit, so I prayed and pled the protection of the blood of Jesus over the plane.

We had a great takeoff from Port Harcourt, and people were relaxed and chatting to one another. After a while, however, we encountered a severe storm and the plane began to shake. All of a sudden, without any warning, the plane suddenly dropped. In an instant, people started screaming. Young and old were crying, and I heard all kinds of prayer that day on the plane.

Someone shouted, "Oh Father, Jesus, Mary help us!"

Others repeated, "Jesus, Jesus, Jesus."

One guy cried, "Mohammed, Mohammed."

I looked at him and said, "Mohammed cannot help you."

One Christian woman panicked and yelled, "Holy Ghost fire, fall on us!"

I yelled, "Shut up, lady. What's wrong with you? We've got rain outside, thunder and lightning, and you want fire inside. Are you nuts?"

The woman sitting next to me grabbed my hands and said, "We're going to die!"

I answered, "Maybe you, but not me. I'm too young to die. God has said He will satisfy me with long life. I am covered with the blood of Jesus, and no weapon formed against me will prosper."

You see, my faith in the protection of the blood and the promises of God was the anchor for my mind. In the natural, I wanted to run around the plane and scream, but at the same time I believed I was protected by the blood of Jesus.

In a matter of time, everything became calm. However, one lady remained so scared that when we finally landed and she got off the plane, she kissed the ground and said, "I'm never going back on a plane again." Personally, I am thankful for the blood of Jesus. Anytime you go anywhere, simply confess the protection of the blood of Jesus.

N) *Boldness*

Having therefore, brethren, boldness to enter into the holiest by the blood of Jesus (Hebrews 10:19).

So, friends, we can now—without hesitation—walk right up to God, into "the Holy Place." Jesus has cleared the way by the blood of His sacrifice, acting as our priest before God. The "curtain" into God's presence is His body (Hebrews 10:19-20 MSG).

It is one thing to have access or an opportunity, but to have boldness to enter the holiest is a different matter. The blood gives you boldness to enter. Boldness means:

- Freedom in speaking, unreservedness in speech.
- Without concealment.
- Free and fearless confidence and assurance.
- The deportment by which one becomes conspicuous or secures publicity.

The blood gives you a fearless entrance before God. It gives:

- Freedom of access.
- Freedom of speech.
- Freedom of movement.

Now if the blood can bring you before God, why should you be afraid to stand before any man or devil? The boldness that you receive from the blood will eliminate and eradicate fear from your life. A revelation of the blood of Jesus will cause you to walk in fearlessness and remove the scent of a prey from you.

The Devil Bought Me a Coke

Although I was raised in England, I was born in Mauritius, and I remember the first time I went back to Mauritius. I was walking along with a friend when we came to a crossroad where somebody had left flowers, money, and a candle on the road. My friend cautioned me, saying, "Better cross the road, Glenn!"

Puzzled, I asked, "Why?"

He stated, "This is witchcraft. Somebody has left this money and some kind of offering in order to hurt someone else."

After listening to his explanation, I decided to continue walking on the same path. I knew the power of the blood of Jesus, and I understood whatever harm this offering was meant to give could not be a factor to my life because I am covered by the blood of Jesus. But as I stayed on course and showed no sign of crossing the road, my friend began to panic and kept repeating things like, "Let's cross the road; we don't know what kind of spell or bad thing will happen."

Then I decided to walk over, kick the flowers, and pick up the money that was on the ground. By this time, my friend was freaking out. I looked at him and said, "The Bible says the wealth of the wicked is laid up for the just. If the devil is stupid enough to leave money on the road, then the righteous will enjoy it." Then I took the money and went into a store, bought a can of Coke, and drank it with enjoyment. Afterward, I said to my bewildered friend, "The devil bought me some Coca Cola today!" Needless to say, he did not see the funny side of this.

A revelation of the blood of Jesus will cause you to walk in fearlessness. My friend was expecting something to happen to both of us. And it did! My thirst was quenched as I enjoyed a cold Coke while he continued to endure a dry throat because he allowed his fear to rule and refused to touch that money. If I had not have understood the authority of the blood of Jesus, I would have also been just as nervous as my friend.

O) *Release of Wealth and Prosperity*

Did you notice that the wealth of Egypt was not transferred and that God's people were not released into wealth until the blood was applied?

> *For the Lord will pass through to smite the Egyptians; and when He seeth the blood upon the lintel, and on the two side posts, the Lord will pass over the door, and will not suffer the destroyer to come in unto your houses to smite you....*
>
> *And he [Pharaoh] called for Moses and Aaron by night, and said, Rise up, and get you forth from among my people, both ye and the children of Israel; and go, serve the Lord, as ye have said. Also take your flocks and your herds, as ye have said, and be gone; and bless me also. And the Egyptians were urgent upon the people, that they might send them out of the land in haste; for they said, We be all dead men. And the people took their dough before it was leavened, their kneadingtroughs being bound up in their clothes upon their shoulders. And the children of Israel did according to the word of Moses; and they borrowed of the Egyptians jewels of silver, and jewels of gold, and raiment: and the Lord gave the people favour in the sight of the Egyptians, so that they lent unto them such things as they required. And they spoiled the Egyptians (Exodus 12:23,31-36).*

Four hundred years of hard labor came to an abrupt end. Years of struggling, never having enough, came to a halt because of the blood application. The withholding of finances from God's people by Egypt came to an end because of the blood. The stubbornness of Pharaoh was relinquished because of the blood. Likewise, every stubborn spirit of poverty in your life will bow before you when you put yourself under the blood of Jesus. All through the plagues of Egypt, Moses continued to say, "Let my people go," but stubborn Pharaoh would not let them go. But when the blood of a lamb was applied, Pharaoh and all of Egypt quickly changed their minds and pleaded with the Hebrew children, "You must leave now!" while gifting them with silver and gold. The same will happen to you. Your days of poverty are over!

P) Restitution

Through the substitutionary work of Jesus on the cross, we receive restitution.

Restitution means:

1. An act of restoring or a condition of being restored: as

    a) a restoration of something to its rightful owner.

    b) a making good of or giving an equivalent for some injury.

2. A legal action serving to cause restoration of a previous state.

Jesus' substitution is my restitution. I have been restored to a place of authority and power because of the blood of Jesus.

> As for thee also, **by the blood of thy covenant** I have sent forth thy prisoners out of the pit wherein is no water. Turn you to the strong hold, ye prisoners of hope: **even today do I declare that I will render double unto thee** (Zechariah 9:11-12).

The blood of Jesus is your access and guarantee to the double portion. Adam had grace but we have more—even a double portion of grace.

Q) Breaking of Generational Curses

Through Adam's transgression, all generations through the ages became sinners, but thank God the curse is broken through the blood of Jesus.

> As the bird by wandering, as the swallow by flying, so **the curse causeless shall not come** (Proverbs 26:2).

> Christ hath **redeemed us from the curse** of the law... (Galatians 3:13).

The cause of the curse was Adam's sin, and the cure for the curse is Jesus' blood. Any generational curse is broken through the application of the blood. The four hundred years of bondage of Israel came to an abrupt end through the blood. Another example of the blood's power to break a generational curse can be seen in the life of Rahab, the harlot. Imminent judgment was heading towards Jericho, and by all accounts, she deserved an appropriate punishment. Yet through protecting the spies whom Joshua sent and hanging the scarlet thread, representing Jesus' blood, outside her window, she and her family were spared from total destruction. The curse came upon everything else but the household of Rahab simply because of the blood.

Two Types of Curses

There are two types of curses—one being generational, meaning from within, and the other an agent, meaning from without. In either case, Jesus' blood is the cure.

A curse is defined as:

1. A malevolent appeal to a supernatural being for harm to come to somebody.

2. A cause of unhappiness or harm.

3. Constant irritation and annoyance.

4. To inflict something unpleasant on somebody.

5. Marked for destruction.

6. Destined to be doomed.

7. To pronounce gloom and doom on the present and future of somebody.

In the present day, many are afraid of curses, yet there is absolutely no need for you to fear any curse. I do not care who or what may come against you, they are helpless against the blood of Jesus. Just because diseases have seemingly been passed down through your family line does not mean that you have to put up with them. Many have given up all hope because cancer, diabetes, arthritis, asthma or other illnesses are prevalent among family members. They have accepted these diseases as part of their genetic makeup and feel helpless to do anything about them. That is a lie from the devil! He would love for you to believe that a curse cannot be broken. The devil is a liar! Jesus' blood paid the price to set you free. You are in Christ and you are now in His line. He has provided divine health, which is your portion today. Identify yourself with Jesus.

The second type of curse is one in which someone invokes wicked spirits to harm a person through pronouncing failures and sacrifices. Many times they come in the form of pronouncements. Whatever the case, a child of God need not fear. A great example of the powerlessness of a pronounced curse can be seen in the Old Testament, when King Balak paid the prophet Balaam to curse Israel.

> *Then the people of Israel traveled to the plains of Moab and camped east of the Jordan River, across from Jericho. Balak son of Zippor, the Moabite king, knew what the Israelites had done to the Amorites. And when they saw how many Israelites there were, he and his people were terrified. The king of Moab said to the leaders of Midian, "This mob will devour everything in sight, like an ox devours grass!" So Balak, king of Moab, sent messengers to Balaam son of Beor, who was living in his native land of Pethor near the Euphrates River. He sent this message to request that Balaam come to help him: "A vast horde of people has arrived from Egypt. They cover the face of the earth and are threatening me. Please come and curse them for me because they are so numerous. Then perhaps I will be able to conquer them and drive them from the land. I know that blessings fall on the people you bless. I also know that the people you curse are doomed." Balak's messengers, officials of both Moab and Midian,* **set out and took money with them to pay Balaam to curse Israel**...(Numbers 22:1-7 NLT).

> *So Balaam returned to the place where the king and the officials of Moab were standing beside Balak's burnt offerings. "What did the Lord say?" Balak asked eagerly. This was the prophecy Balaam delivered: "Rise up, Balak, and listen! Hear me, son of Zippor. God is not a man, that He should lie. He is not a human, that He should change His mind. Has He ever spoken and failed to act? Has He ever promised and not carried it through?* **I received a command to bless; He has blessed, and I cannot reverse it!** *No misfortune is in sight for Jacob; no trouble is in store for Israel. For the Lord their God is with them; He has been proclaimed their king. God has brought them out of Egypt; He is like a strong ox for them. No curse can touch Jacob; no sorcery has any power against Israel. For now it will be said of Jacob, 'What wonders God has done for Israel!' These people rise up like a lioness; like a majestic lion they stand..."* (Numbers 23:17-24 NLT).

I want you to notice, even though sacrifices and a prophet were involved, nothing could harm the people of God. The Scriptures are very clear concerning pronounced curses:

1. God has blessed and no one can reverse it.

2. No misfortune is in sight for Jacob.

3. No trouble is in store for Israel.

4. No curse can touch Jacob.

5. No sorcery has any power against Israel.

Whereas these people were under the old covenant, we have an even better covenant established upon better promises; therefore, how much more are we protected? Even the old patriarch Job knew of this protection:

Thou shalt be hid from the scourge of the tongue: neither shalt thou be afraid of destruction when it cometh (Job 5:21).

You will be protected from the tongue that strikes like a whip, and you will not be afraid when destruction comes (Job 5:21 NCV).

Too Much Blood

As I mentioned previously, I travel extensively, ministering the Gospel to the nations of the world. And while I love the American flair and enthusiasm for church and I compassionately feel that Europe desperately needs a touch from God, I have always found Africa and the islands to be the most fascinating and exciting. People there are very bold in their worship and dedication to God or the devil. Witches have even come to my meetings to attempt to do me harm, but instead were saved by the blood of Jesus.

I will never forget the time when I was ministering in an African nation, teaching and praying for the sick and some witches showed up to disturb the meetings. I did not panic because I am aware that I am blessed of the Lord and I am in agreement with what the scriptures say, *"He* [God] *hath blessed; and I cannot reverse it"* (Num. 23:20). I knew the blood of Jesus is too much for any curse that the enemy may send against me. There is no mystery to it—simply agree with what the Word says and no curse can attach itself to you.

Because of the blood of Jesus, I expect:

1. To be blessed. No one can reverse that fact.

2. No sorcery or witchcraft can touch me.

3. No trouble, misfortune, or curse can be effective against me.

R) Deliverance and Hope

Rejoice greatly, O daughter of Zion; shout, O daughter of Jerusalem: behold, thy King cometh unto thee: He is just, and having salvation; lowly, and riding upon an ass, and upon a colt the foal of an ass.

And I will cut off the chariot from Ephraim, and the horse from Jerusalem, and the battle bow shall be cut off: and He shall speak peace unto the heathen: and His dominion shall be from sea even to sea, and from river even to the ends of the earth.

As for thee also, by the blood of thy covenant I have sent forth thy prisoners out of the pit wherein is no water.

Turn you to the strong hold, ye prisoners of hope: ***even today do I declare that I will render double unto thee*** (Zechariah 9:9-12).

Just as Israel's four hundred years of slavery ended with the blood, so has satan's dominion over humanity ended with the blood of Jesus. There is always deliverance from the taskmaster of life through the blood. The blood gave hope to Israel in Egypt, and the blood of Jesus is our hope in this world.

The Night I Will Never Forget

In the Introduction of this book, I made mention of my granddad, a great man, whom we called "Pador." When we were young, my brother and I used to ask him to tell us ghost stories at nighttime, and I remember that my hair would stand up when he told us some of the things he had seen. Even though these stories would freak me out, I remained still and listened intently. Looking back now, I realized that was a stupid thing to do. At the end of the story, he would say, "Go close the window."

I would squeal, "I'm not going anywhere." (I was scared spitless!)

"In fact, Pador, I am sleeping next to you tonight!"

As a little child, I was gripped and held prisoner by a spirit of fear. On the outside, I was a happy-go-lucky person, but on the inside I was terrified of certain things. For instance, I was afraid of going to hell! As an 8 year old, I had asked about the endtimes. I had heard that Jesus was coming on a white horse and whoever did not belong to Him was going to hell. I cried and cried, "Mom, I don't want to go to hell!" She did not know how to handle my distress and simply replied, "Be a good boy." Then I really knew I was doomed to hell. In the meantime, my brother Bruno enjoyed seeing me cry my eyes out.

Furthermore, I was afraid of demon spirits! In Mauritius, my neighbors were good people but practiced an eastern religion. I witnessed their sacrifices and festivals, which freaked me out. One time I awoke at three o'clock in the morning and heard loud footsteps outside. The steps sounded like a person walking who was wearing metal soles. They kept going round and round the yard. When I woke up later that morning, I asked my granddad what the sound was. He nonchalantly replied, "That's the guardian spirit that the neighbors worship walking around."

"Oh God, why did I ask?" That was just too much information for a kid. I could not go to sleep that night, and guess what happened again at three o'clock in the morning? I heard those stinking steps. I was going out of my mind. Mauritius is a hot tropical island, and Port Louis is like living in an oven. Even so, I covered my head with a blanket, although I was soaked with sweat, and my heart beat faster and faster. In addition, Bruno had a habit of humming in his sleep—humming that was long and loud. How could I ever sleep with Frankenstein outside and his buddy "hummingboy" inside? I wanted to get up and slap my brother, but I was too scared to remove the blanket and see you-know-who! For a long time, I was scared to death of nighttime. Then we moved to London, England—no more footsteps outside, and because I had a room of my own, there was no more humming inside.

After ten years living in the United Kingdom, I returned for a visit to Mauritius in 1993. I went to bed, and guess what I heard at three o'clock in the morning? Footsteps! But this time, it was different. I was saved, filled with the Holy Ghost, and covered by the blood. I said to myself, "I cannot go to sleep with that stupid noise outside!" I got up, opened the window, and yelled, "I take authority over you in the name of Jesus and by the power of His blood. Get away from here. I plead the blood and draw a bloodline. Now, satan, get lost." That was the end of footsteps.

S) Empowerment to Do the Will of God

*Now the God of peace, that brought again from the dead our Lord Jesus, that great shepherd of the sheep, **through the blood of the everlasting covenant, make you perfect in every good work to do His will,** working in you that which is wellpleasing in His sight, through Jesus Christ; to whom be glory for ever and ever. Amen* (Hebrews 13:20-21).

The blood of Jesus will complete you and equip you so that you can do what God has called you to do. If His blood was sufficient to take you in His salvation will, then His blood is sufficient to take you into His ministry and personal will of God for your life.

T) Healing and Divine Health

One of the greatest benefits of the blood of Jesus is divine health. In fact, this is the divine right of every believer. Look at what is said of Israel when they were leaving Egypt:

*He smote also all the firstborn in their land [Egypt], the chief of all their strength. He brought them [Israel] forth also with silver and gold: and **there was not one feeble person among their tribes** (Psalm 105:36-37).*

*Then He led the Israelites out; they carried silver and gold, **and all of them were healthy and strong** (Psalm 105:37 GNB).*

Can you imagine—God kept over two million people in divine health through the blood. If God can do that in the old covenant, then He can also surely do it in the new covenant. It is your right to be healthy. The same blood that paid for your sins also paid for your healing.

*Who His own self bare our sins in His own body on the tree, that we, being dead to sins, should live unto righteousness: **by whose stripes ye were healed** (1 Peter 2:24).*

Healing is in our redemption! If sickness came through the fall, then healing comes with salvation. God's work in Christ Jesus is more powerful than the work of satan in Adam. There is no need for the believer to put up with ill heath when Jesus paid the price for your health.

Everyone wants to walk in divine health. As you read this book, it may be that you need the touch of God in your body or one of your loved ones needs healing. Whatever the case, rest assured that there is hope in God and His Word! What you are reading is no accident. God wants you well more than you desire to be well. First, you need to understand there are three beliefs when it comes to the subject of divine healing.

1. *Healing is passed away*. There is a belief that the miracle of healing is no longer viable today. However, this thinking is totally ludicrous, absurd, and illogical. God instigates healing. He is the healer. Healing did not pass away with the apostles. Jesus is the Apostle of our faith, and healing is not passed away.

2. *Special grace*. This means it may happen sometimes, or it may not. It all depends upon the sovereignty of God. He may decide to heal one and refuse to heal another, maybe just to teach a lesson. That is a faith-sapping concept and is straight from the pit of hell. This belief cannot be valid because after studying the New Testament, you cannot find one occasion where Jesus refused to heal somebody. The Scriptures reveal that He healed all who came to Him. He never once said, "According to the sovereignty of God, you are healed," but "According to your faith, be it done unto you" or "Your faith hath made you whole."

3. *Healing is part of our redemption* belonging to every believer, as it is God's will. Some theologians called it, "Healing in the atonement." You have a God-given right to be well. *Does our redemption in Christ provide bodily healing?* Yes, it does. Is healing part of our salvation? Yes—emphatically yes! Do not let the devil or some unbelieving preacher talk you out of your covenant rights in Christ Jesus. At the cross, Jesus shed His blood, paid for the salvation of your spirit and healing of your body, and you should hold strong to that truth! *The suffering, death, and resurrection of Jesus Christ purchased your physical healing.*

When it comes to healing, as you study the Word, you will find there are three stages:

1. *Divine healing.*

   This is wonderful news! During this initial stage, you first hear about healing, and that it is available to you. You can receive it through the laying on of hands, prayer of faith, or anointing with oil. It comes as you seek God for healing for your sickness or disability.

2. *Divine health.*

   Divine healing is good, but divine health is better. During this stage, the believer maintains his healing and continues to walk in health. The apostle John desired that we walk in this truth.

   Beloved, I wish above all things that thou mayest prosper and be in health, even as thy soul prospereth (3 John 2).

3. *Divine life.*

   Divine life is the highest form of health, and it is for the whole person—spirit, soul, and body. Jesus said, *"I am come that* [you] *might have life, and...have it more abundantly"* (John 10:10b). The Greek word for "life" is zoe, meaning the God-kind of life or the high life. Moses told us the life is in the blood. Divine health is in divine life, which is in divine blood.

The Devil Is a Liar

Do not buy the lies that satan has sold to others. If you have been in the church long enough, you have already heard reasons why healing is not for today. These reasons are lies from the devil. Some will even tell you that it is God's will for you to be sick and that you bring glory to Him when you accept it. Nothing could be further from the truth. People who reason like that have no understanding of the power of the blood and the power of covenant. Note this powerful revelation and allow it to penetrate your mind and spirit: Even as it is the will of God for everyone to be saved, it is also the will of God for everyone to be healed. Someone may say, "Not everyone will be healed." Well, neither are all men saved, but it does not change the fact that God sent Jesus to the cross to bring salvation to *all* men.

*...this is good and acceptable in the sight of God our Saviour; **who will have all men to be saved**, and to come unto the knowledge of the truth* (1 Timothy 2:3-4).

Is it God's will for all men to be saved? Of course it is. The Bible states, *"Whosoever shall call upon the name of the Lord shall be saved"* (Rom. 10:13).

Nobody in their right mind would deny that God wants to save all men. That being true, what does the word save mean? It means to be whole and sound in your entire being. He wants your spirit saved, your mind renewed, and your body well. You are to bring God glory in your being as you belong to God.

> *For God bought you with a high price. So you must honor God with your body* (1 Corinthians 6:20 NLT).

> *For ye are bought with a price: therefore glorify God in your body, and in your spirit, which are God's* (1 Corinthians 6:20).

You do not glorify God in your body when you are sick; you glorify God when you are well and healed, as we notice. in the lives of people in the Gospels:

> *Insomuch that the multitude wondered, when they saw the dumb to speak, the maimed to be whole, the lame to walk, and the blind to see: and they **glorified** the God of Israel* (Matthew 15:31).

> *And immediately he arose, took up the bed, and went forth before them all; insomuch that they were all amazed, and **glorified** God, saying, We never saw it on this fashion* (Mark 2:12).

> *And He laid his hands on her: and immediately she was made straight, and **glorified** God* (Luke 13:13).

The people glorified God when they were healed. You, likewise, bring glory to God when you walk in divine health. Your life should constantly be radiating divine health because Jesus paid for your health with His blood, a very costly price that we cannot overlook or ignore.

U) The Blood Whitens

> [They] *have washed their robes, and made them white in the blood of the Lamb* (Revelation 7:14).

The believer and his garments are made white. This is not referring to skin color but our status or standing in God. The same word *white* is used to refer to the clothing of Jesus during His transfiguration (see Matt. 17:2) and to the garments of the 24 elders around the throne.

*And round about the throne were four and twenty seats: and upon the seats I saw four and twenty elders sitting, **clothed in white raiment**; and they had on their heads crowns of gold* (Revelation 4:4).

We see the word *white* also used to describe the clothing of the angel at the resurrection (see Matt. 28:3). The blood of Jesus gives us a holy covering, whereas the Bible says that our garments and "righteousness are filthy rags."

*But we are all as an unclean thing, and all our righteousnesses are as **filthy rags**; and we all do fade as a leaf; and our iniquities, like the wind, have taken us away* (Isaiah 64:6).

We cannot enter God's house with our own covering as it is unclean. However, Jesus' blood gives us a clean covering, removing the darkness of sin and impurity from our lives.

May God Himself, the God who makes everything holy and whole, make you holy and whole, put you together—spirit, soul, and body—and keep you fit for the coming of our Master, Jesus Christ (1 Thessalonians 5:23 MSG).

V) Habitation of the Spirit

Through the blood, our bodies now have become the temple of the Holy Spirit. In the Old Testament, God was *for* His people and *with* His people, but could not be *in* His people. In the New Testament, as a result of the blood of Jesus, God is *for* us, He is *with* us, and thank God, He is *in* us.

For ye are bought with a price: therefore glorify God in your body, and in your spirit, which are God's (1 Corinthians 6:20).

Paul says, "You are bought with a price." What price? The blood. And the only way we can be fit to be inhabited by the Holy Spirit is after the blood has washed us.

And from Jesus Christ, who is the faithful witness, and the first begotten of the dead, and the prince of the kings of the earth. Unto Him that loved us, and washed us from our sins in His own blood (Revelation 1:5).

W) Right to Use the Name of Jesus

One of the customary rituals that covenant partners performed when entering a blood covenant was the exchanging of names. Both partners could add the other's name to his or hers, or just one would take the other's name. We see this in marriage today. When God made a covenant with Abram, his name was then changed to Abraham, and his wife Sarai's name was changed to Sarah. God added His own name to Abraham's, and God, in turn, was known as the God of Abraham. Today we are called by the name of Jesus, having the legal right to His name. This is called power of attorney. The blood of Jesus has authorized us to use His name, in which there is authority and power. In fact, according to the apostle Peter, His name is now the believer's inheritance.

> Then Peter said, Silver and gold have I none; **but such as I have give I thee: In the name of Jesus Christ of Nazareth** rise up and walk (Acts 3:6).

The name of Jesus is your covenant name. There are signs, wonders, and miracles in that name. Jesus told us, *"In My name, shall they cast out devils…"* (Mark 16:17b).

X) Right to Wear the Armor of God

Do you realize because of the blood we are able to wear the armor of God? Giving and receiving armor was part of the ceremony of a blood covenant, as demonstrated when David and Jonathan exchanged their weapons.

> Then Jonathan and David **made a covenant**, because he loved him as his own soul. And Jonathan stripped himself of the robe that was upon him, **and gave it to David, and his garments, even to his sword, and to his bow, and to his girdle** (1 Samuel 18:3-4).

The exchanging of weapons speaks volumes in covenant. It is saying, "I am your strength and protection." In giving you my weapons, I am saying to you I will protect you with my life. These weapons at our disposal are not carnal but spiritual which will bring destruction to satan and his cohorts. When you think about it, God did not give you His Sunday clothes but His fighting suit. And when you stand in battle against demons, wearing His armor, those demons consider themselves to be fighting against God. Jesus has already tried these weapons and has over-come the realm and authority of darkness with them.

> *And He saw that there was no man, and wondered that there was no intercessor: therefore His arm brought salvation unto Him; and His righteousness, it sustained Him.*

> *For He put on righteousness as a breastplate, and an helmet of salvation upon His head; and He put on the **garments of vengeance for clothing**, and was clad with zeal as a cloak* (Isaiah 59:16-17).

I want you to note the armor was called the "garments of vengeance." That word in the Hebrew language also means, "punishment." We are not to avenge ourselves against people, but you definitely have the right to punish the devil. He is your enemy; and be warned that if you do not punish him, he will take the opportunity to do so to you. The armor of God is offensive as well as defensive.

Brighton International Believer's Convention

I will never forget the first Kenneth Copeland Believers' Convention I attended in the late '80s. Today, with the numerous Christian TV channels and Internet explosion, we have access to great ministries, but there was a time when we could listen to Brother Kenneth Copeland and others only through tapes or by reading books. So it was a great privilege and an exciting adventure to attend a convention and listen, in person, to a man of God of that caliber. At that time, I was 18 years old. I had grown up listening to him, and I did not want to miss him when he came to the United Kingdom.

So, a few of my friends and I got together and drove to the convention in a minibus. We had no money for hotels and declared, "If we have to sleep on the floor, we will do it." And we did. We slept on the floor of a church, but we did not mind. We were young and hungry for the Word.

The first night, the atmosphere was electric as people praised and worshipped God. When the Word came, I was so charged up, I felt I could walk through walls and eat nails. My only disappointment was sitting in the balcony far away from the front line. I thought to myself, *Man, I didn't come this far to be stuck up here in the balcony. Tomorrow I will be in the front!* If you have ever been to a Believers' meeting, you know that only ministers can sit in the front, but somehow in the next evening service, I found myself in the front seat. I wore blue Adidas tennis shoes, a T-shirt, Levi jeans, and a jacket—not the traditional minister's look, but I did not care. I was happy and could not wait for Brother Copeland to show up for the preaching after the praise and worship.

Everything was terrific. I was basking in the presence of God, and when he showed up, he led us in worshiping in the Spirit, which was great. Then all of a sudden, there was a ruckus. At first, I did not pay any attention, but then the noise came closer. It was a little demon-possessed woman, screaming, picking up things, and throwing them. My first thought was, *Oh God, I hope she does not come near me, pick me up, and throw me.* As she came closer to the front, she threw herself on the floor and was writhing like a snake. Then she looked at me and stuck her tongue out. In the back of my mind, I was thinking, *Stupid, stupid, you couldn't stay happy in the balcony. No, you wanted to be in front. Now you have to deal with snake-woman.* Right then, the balcony really appealed me. While all this was going on, Brother Copeland who was on the platform, looked down and said, "Don't be afraid!" My thought was, *That's easy for you to say. You come down here and I'll go up there; then we'll see about not being afraid.* His next statement gave me a revelation of the armor of God. He said, "Satan cannot see you."

I thought, *What! Are you kidding? Not only has he seen me, but he poked his tongue out at me.*

He continued, "You are wearing the armor of God. Satan does not know if it's you or God standing there. Your legs might be shaking on the inside, but he cannot see you as long as you have your armor on." Then all of a sudden, fear dissipated and boldness came. I have never forgotten that! The reason you and I can wear the armor of God today is because of the blood of Jesus.

Υ) *A Friend of God*

It is by virtue of the blood of Jesus that we can be called a friend of God. The word *friend* is actually a covenant term. Today we use the term too loosely. It is more than just a mere acquaintance. Jesus gave His blood and life for us; hence, He can be called our friend. Actually, there are two Hebrew words for the term *friend* that we must pay attention to. The first word is rea or rayah, meaning associate or companion.

A *friend loveth at all times, and a brother is born for adversity* (Proverbs 17:17).

A *man that hath friends must show himself friendly: and there is a friend that sticketh closer than a brother* (Proverbs 18:24).

The second Hebrew word for *friend* is the word *ahab,* and it is this word that is used when the Bible says, *"…there is a friend that sticketh closer than a brother."* This kind of friend is a blood covenant friend. This relationship is stronger than the relationship of two brothers from the same mother's womb and who drank from the same breast. There is a saying in the West, "Blood is thicker than water," similar to one in the East, "Blood is thicker than milk."

"Blood is thicker than milk" means that blood covenant relation is a stronger tie than the relationship of milk brothers who were fed from the same breast. No one has a choice as to who their natural siblings are, but you can choose your covenant friend and brother. "Blood is thicker than water" also has the same connotation, referring to the breaking of waters to bring forth children. The children who have come from the same womb are not as closely knit in their hearts as those of a blood covenant-friend relationship. This kind of friend loves at all times. He is dependable, trustworthy, and loyal. He will never leave you nor forsake you. He is there in the storm and in the good times. In fact, he will lay down his life to bring the good times to his covenant friend.

Faithful *are the wounds of a friend, but the kisses of an enemy are deceitful* (Proverbs 27:6).

Jesus is our friend whose wounds are faithful to cleanse us and restore us into relationship with the Most High God.

Abraham was also known as a friend of God because of his blood covenant relationship.

Art *not Thou our God, who didst drive out the inhabitants of this land before Thy people Israel, and gavest it to the seed of* **Abraham Thy friend** *for ever?* (2 Chronicles 20:7).

But *thou, Israel, art My servant, Jacob whom I have chosen, the seed of Abraham My friend* (Isaiah 41:8).

God moved on behalf of Abraham in extraordinary fashion. He helped him in battle to win what looked like an impossible battle against Chedorlaomer (see Gen. 14). The apostle Paul tells us in Galatians that if we belong to God, then we are Abraham's seed. Therefore, today, you and I are friends of God.

> *Henceforth I call you not servants; for the servant knoweth not what his lord doeth: but I have called you friends; for all things that I have heard of My Father I have made known unto you* (John 15:15).

Z) The End of Ceremonial Sacrifices

Thank God for the blood of Jesus, which brought to an end the daily and yearly ceremonial sacrifices of the temple. The blood of Jesus was shed to finally satisfy the just demands of the law.

> *For such an high priest became us, who is holy, harmless, undefiled, separate from sinners, and made higher than the heavens;* **who needeth not daily**, *as those high priests, to offer up sacrifice, first for his own sins, and then for the people's: for this He did once, when He offered up Himself* (Hebrews 7:26-27).

> *For the law having a shadow of good things to come, and not the very image of the things,* **can never with those sacrifices which they offered year by year continually make the comers thereunto perfect**.

> **For then would they not have ceased to be offered?** *because that the worshippers once purged should have had no more conscience of sins.*

> *But in those sacrifices there is a remembrance again made of sins every year.*

> *For it is not possible that the blood of bulls and of goats should take away sins* (Hebrews 10:1-4).

> *For Christ is the end of the law for righteousness to every one that believeth* (Romans 10:4).

Just before Jesus died on the cross, He cried, "It is finished." He did not say, "I am finished," but "It is finished." What was finished? The rites and the sacrifices. All the animals slain in the Old Testament were pointing to the Perfect One who would come one day and put an end

74

to all sacrifices. "It is finished" was not an expression of failure from the lips of Jesus but an expression of victory. In Greek, it is the word *Tetelestai*, and it had a twofold meaning.

1. A receipt stamped with the words "paid in full" was a receipt given when someone paid their bill in the marketplace and they would run through the streets shouting "Tetelestai, tetelestai." Prisoners who served their time would have the receipt posted on the door of their house to indicate they had paid the price. When Jesus said, "It is finished," He was saying the debt was paid. He was referring to the debt of our sins. Jesus paid the debt for our sins in full on the cross.

2. A shout of victory was heard after two gladiators fought in the arena. One would win and one would die. Before the conquering gladiator would thrust his sword into the throat of the defeated one, he would say, "Tetelestai." It was the shout of the conqueror.

> It is finished—death has been conquered.
> It is finished—the blood has conquered.
> It is finished—satan's grip is broken.
> It is finished—the price is paid in full.
> It is finished—you are free.

Jesus Paid It All

I hear the Savior say,
"Thy strength indeed is small;
Child of weakness, watch and pray,
Find in Me thine all in all."

Jesus paid it all,
All to Him I owe;
Sin had left a crimson stain,
He washed it white as snow.

For nothing good have I
Whereby Thy grace to claim,
I'll wash my garments white
In the blood of Calv'ry's Lamb.

And now complete in Him
My robe His righteousness,
Close sheltered 'neath His side,
I am divinely blest.

Lord, now indeed I find
Thy power and Thine alone,
Can change the leper's spots
And melt the heart of stone.

When from my dying bed
My ransomed soul shall rise,
"Jesus died my soul to save,"
Shall rend the vaulted skies.

And when before the throne
I stand in Him complete,
I'll lay my trophies down
All down at Jesus' feet.

CHAPTER 5

The Sevenfold Blessings of the Shed Blood

We now know and understand that the shed blood of the Savior is the reason for our redemption. Our freedom could not be a reality had Jesus not willingly offered Himself as the ultimate sacrifice. In this chapter, we will look at seven blessings of the blood. In the Bible, the number *seven* stands for completion and perfection, and in the Old Testament, the high priest sprinkled the sacrificial blood seven times.

> *And he shall take of the blood of the bullock, and sprinkle it with his finger upon the mercy seat eastward; and* **before the mercy seat shall he sprinkle of the blood with his finger seven times** (Leviticus 16:14).

In the Word, there are seven ways that Jesus shed His blood. These ways are very important to our understanding and walking in freedom and authority. Let's take a look at them and how they affect our lives.

Seven Blood Offerings

Circumcision

> *And when eight days were accomplished for the circumcising of the child, His name was called Jesus, which was so named of the angel before He was conceived in the womb* (Luke 2:21).

It is obvious that the first time Jesus' blood was spilled on the earth was during circumcision. Paul reveals in his Galatians Epistle the implication of this act: *"For I testify again to every man that is circumcised, that he is a debtor to do the whole law"* (Gal. 5:3). We know no man has ever kept every jot and tittle of the law. It has been impossible for any fallen man to succeed in this area; however, Jesus said He did not come to break the law but to fulfill it.

> *Think not that I am come to destroy the law, or the prophets: I am not come to destroy, but to fulfill* (Matthew 5:17).

Paul said if a man is circumcised, he is obligated to keep the law, whereas Jesus said He came to fulfill the law. Jesus' circumcision reveals that He was willing to keep the law, and He did so perfectly, whereas you and I could never keep the law. Yet today we live in what Jesus fulfilled. I am not saved by my good works but by His good works.

Sweating at the Garden of Gethsemane

On His way to Calvary, the first place Jesus shed His blood was in the Garden of Gethsemane just after what is commonly known as the Last Supper. Interestingly, Adam lost his battle in one garden, and Jesus won His battle in another garden.

> *Then cometh Jesus with them unto a place called Gethsemane, and saith unto the disciples, Sit ye here, while I go and pray yonder.*
>
> *And He took with Him Peter and the two sons of Zebedee, and began to be sorrowful and very heavy.*
>
> *Then saith He unto them, My soul is exceeding sorrowful, even unto death: tarry ye here, and watch with Me.*
>
> *And He went a little farther, and fell on His face, and prayed, saying, O My Father, if it be possible, let this cup pass from Me: nevertheless not as I will, but as Thou wilt* (Matthew 26:36-39).
>
> *And being in an agony He prayed more earnestly: and* **His sweat was as it were great drops of blood falling down to the ground** (Luke 22:44).

The medical term, *hematidrosis*, is a very rare condition in which a human being sweats blood. It can occur when a person is suffering extreme levels of stress, as in facing his or her own death, which causes the capillaries to break in the sweat glands. I want to remind you that Jesus did nothing for Himself but everything for us. He faced extreme stress so that you and I could be free from stress. *You can have a stress-free life.*

He was in agony so that you and I can be free from agony. The pressure upon Him was immense, yet He never bowed before satan. He said, *"...not as I will, but as You will, Father"* (see Luke 22:42). You do not have to break down under pressure. I am not underestimating your problem, but I assure you it is incomparable to Jesus' testings. You have never faced pressure like Jesus did. Yet He passed, and you can also pass through. Jesus is your burden-remover and yoke-destroyer. Cast your burdens upon Him! Unload your concerns, worries, and anxieties upon Him.

Gethsemane, which means "oil press," reveals that you can be free from:

- Stress.
- Fear.
- Panic attack.
- Fretfulness.
- Insanity.
- Losing your mind.

His Back Beaten at the Whipping Post

Everything that the Lord suffered was for our benefit. Jesus also shed His blood at the whipping post where Pilate had Him flogged. This was not just a couple of lashes with a stick, but a brutal attack on the body.

*And as they were eating, Jesus took bread, and blessed it, and **brake** it, and gave it to the disciples, and said, Take, eat; this is My body* (Matthew 26:26).

Jesus Himself said His body was broken for our benefits.

Then Pilate therefore took Jesus, and scourged Him (John 19:1).

Roman scourging normally consisted of 39 lashes and sometimes more. According to custom, a condemned criminal would be scourged before he was put to death. The Roman scourge, also known as the flagrum or flagellum, was a short whip made of two or three leather (ox-hide) thongs or ropes connected to a handle. The rope was knotted with a number of small pieces of metal and bones at various intervals. Scourging or whipping would violently rip the skin. Torn flesh, deep cuts, exposed muscles, and excessive bleeding would leave the person half-dead. Although it was the intention to keep the criminal alive to be crucified, many times the criminal died from such ruthless beatings.

As the custom was, Jesus' hands would have been tied to the whipping post and His back, buttocks, and legs would have been exposed to the person whipping as well as to the audience. It was a shameful and brutal experience. The beatings tore His back, buttocks, legs, and muscle tissues, causing excessive bleeding and hypovolemic shock. This means that the person would lose a large volume of blood causing the heart to beat faster in order to pump blood that was not there. Secondly, the loss of blood would result in a drop of blood pressure causing dizziness, fainting, and collapse. Thirdly, the kidneys would stop producing urine to maintain the remainder of blood volume. Fourthly, the person would become extremely thirsty as the body craved fluids to replace the blood loss.

> I **gave My back** to the smiters, and My cheeks to them that plucked off the hair: I hid not My face from shame and spitting (Isaiah 50:6).

Jesus did all this for my welfare. He did this so I can be healed today! The apostle Peter said, *"By [His] stripes ye were healed"* (1 Pet. 2:24b). Jesus took those stripes so that you could be free from sickness. I remember being taught in church, as a teenage believer, that there are 39 root causes of all diseases. We could say that Jesus took 39 lashes so that we can be free from all sickness and disease today. You can be free from disease today!

You can be free from blood diseases.

You can be free from cancer.

You can be free from heart failure.

You can be free from low and high blood pressure.

You can be free from muscular dystrophy.

The whipping post is your healing post.

The blood of Jesus is the guarantee for our healing!

His Head Bore a Crown of Thorns

The head of Jesus also bled for our deliverance. You need to realize that Jesus suffered from His head to His feet so that we can be free from our head to our feet. There are several references in the Scriptures that tell us that Jesus' head endured brutal beatings.

> And when they had **plaited a crown of thorns, they put it upon His head**, and a reed in His right hand: and they bowed the knee before Him, and mocked Him, saying, Hail, King of the Jews!
>
> And they spit upon Him, and took the reed, and smote Him on the head (Matthew 27:29-30).
>
> And some began to spit on Him, and to cover His face, and to buffet Him, and to say unto Him, Prophesy: and the servants did strike Him with the palms of their hands (Mark 14:65).

Regarding "thorns" in the Scripture, we learn that they are connected to curses, poverty, and painful work.

> And unto Adam [God] said, Because thou hast hearkened unto the voice of thy wife, and hast eaten of the tree, of which I commanded thee, saying, Thou shalt not eat of it: **cursed is the ground for thy sake; in sorrow shalt thou eat** of it all the days of thy life; **thorns also and thistles shall it bring forth to thee**; and thou shalt eat the herb of the field; in the **sweat of thy face** shalt thou eat bread...(Genesis 3:17-19).

Jesus bore the curse so that you can be free. Paul said that Jesus was made poor so we can become rich (see 2 Cor. 8:9). Now don't get the idea that Jesus walked around in poverty during His earthly life. He was not a poor man. Jesus Himself said, *"You always have the poor with you, but you will not always have Me"* (Matt. 26:11; John 12:8; author's paraphrase). He distinctly clarified that he was not a poor man. Rather, He became poor on the cross where He also became sin for us and bore the curse. There is no need to take a vow of poverty that supposedly will bring pleasure to God. It may sound religious, but in God's eyes it is a vow of stupidity. *Poverty is not a blessing!* According to the Book of Deuteronomy, it is a curse:

> Cursed shall be thy basket and thy store....

And thy heaven that is over thy head shall be brass, and the earth that is under thee shall be iron....

And thou shalt grope at noonday, as the blind gropeth in darkness, and **thou shalt not prosper**...(Deuteronomy 28:17, 23, 29).

Therefore shalt thou serve thine enemies which the Lord shall send against thee, **in hunger, and in thirst, and in nakedness, and in want of all things**... (Deuteronomy 28:48).

Jesus took the curse of poverty and pain for you. Poverty is associated with pain and despair. It causes depression and stress in people's minds and marriages. God's Word says, *"Christ hath redeemed us from the curse of the law..."* (Gal. 3:13). All pain associated with poverty has been dealt with by Jesus' crown of thorns.

You need not be broke today!

You do not have to suffer from migraine headaches.

You do not have to be depressed.

You do not have to suffer from low self-esteem.

You do not have to work two jobs and still find that you cannot make ends meet.

The curse is broken; you are free!

You do not have to sweat to be blessed anymore. You are blessed because of what Jesus did.

His Hands Nailed to the Cross

The fifth place where Jesus shed His blood was His hands when they drove the Roman spikes through them. In the Word, "hands" are associated with impartation and transmission. Jacob blessed the sons of Joseph by laying hands on them. The high priest would lay his hands on the sin offering to transfer the sins of the nation upon it. Through the law of contact and transmission, Israel's sins were transferred. After Adam sinned, we all had guilty hands, whereas only the hands of Jesus could do good and relieve sick and hurting people from their ailments without any cost. Healing, comfort, deliverance, and anointing were released through His hands. Peter told Cornelius that Jesus went about doing good and healing all those oppressed of the devil (see Acts

10:38). When Jesus laid hands on Peter's mother-in-law, she was healed of fever. Death bowed and submitted to life when Jesus laid hands on Jairus' daughter. And the spikes in His hands continue to release His blood and life to us.

His Feet Nailed to the Cross

The sixth place Jesus' blood was shed was when the Roman soldiers nailed His feet to the cross. Remember that because we are the Body of Christ, we have the same authority that He has. Paul's prayer for the Ephesian saints reveals the importance of feet:

> *Cease not to give thanks for you, making mention of you in my prayers....And what is the exceeding greatness of His power to us-ward who believe, according to the working of His mighty power,*
>
> *which He wrought in Christ, when He raised Him from the dead, and set Him at His own right hand in the heavenly places, far above all principality, and power, and might, and dominion, and every name that is named, not only in this world, but also in that which is to come:*
>
> *and hath put **all things under His feet**, and gave Him to be **the head over all things to the church**,*
>
> *which is His body, the fulness of Him that filleth all in all* (Ephesians 1:16,19-23).

All things are under the feet of Jesus, and because we are His Body, all things are under our feet too. Because Jesus' feet were nailed, we can now nail the head of satan. We have authority, dominion, and power because of the feet of Jesus. Notice what the apostle Paul says:

> *And the God of peace shall bruise satan under your feet shortly...* (Romans 16:20).

It is interesting to note that God prophesied to satan in Eden that the Seed of the woman, Jesus, would bruise his head with His feet, and we do the same thing today. Jesus' feet have restored us to dominion and inheritance.

> *Every place whereon the soles of your feet shall tread shall be yours...* (Deuteronomy 11:24).

There is only one place fit for the devil and his cohorts—that's under your feet! You were not created by God to be under the feet of sickness and disease; you are not to be under the feet of witchcraft. You are the head and not the tail. Every devil must be under your feet.

Paul in his letter to the Corinthian church said that history and events recorded in the Old Testament are our example (see 1 Cor. 10:11). Here's one of these examples on which to base your own life:

> And it came to pass, when they brought out those kings unto Joshua, that Joshua called for all the men of Israel, and said unto the captains of the men of war which went with him, Come near, **put your feet upon the necks of these kings**. And they came near, and put their feet upon the necks of them. And Joshua said unto them, Fear not, nor be dismayed, be strong and of good courage: for thus shall the Lord do to all your enemies against whom ye fight (Joshua 10:24-25).

Joshua was a type and shadow of our Lord Jesus Christ. He told his men to put their feet on the necks of their enemies. Jesus is telling you the same thing today—put your foot on the devil's neck.

Put your foot on cancer.

Put your foot on arthritis.

Put your foot on depression.

Today, your feet are shod with the Gospel of peace, and you also can lead others out of their miseries. The Word says, "...How beautiful are the feet of them that preach the gospel of peace..." (Rom. 10:15). The word "beautiful" does not refer to pretty feet, but literally means "timely and in season." The feet of Jesus were timely for us and brought us into our season of dominion. We are no longer in the season of failure and calamity but in the season of power. The season of powerlessness that Adam brought upon mankind has been replaced by the feet of Jesus.

I dare you—put your foot on the devil's neck.

His Pierced Side

Jesus also shed His blood when the soldier pierced His side, which caused blood and water to come forth.

> But when they came to Jesus and saw that He was dead already, they brake not His legs: but one of **the soldiers with a spear**

84

pierced His side, and forthwith came there out blood and water (John 19:33-34).

I want you to note the connection between the water that flowed from His pierced side and Jesus' words in the Gospel of John: *"In the last day, that great day of the feast, Jesus stood and cried, saying, If any man thirst, let him come unto Me, and drink. He that believeth on Me, as the scripture hath said, out of his belly shall flow rivers of living water"* (John 7:37-38). Although many have interpreted the Scripture in John chapter 19 as Jesus dying of a broken and ruptured heart, I also believe it is the sign of new life. Blood and water are evident with the arrival of a newborn. Likewise, the birth of a believer, which has become a reality for untold millions of people all over the world, represents new life and living water. He died to give us life.

Seven Revelations to the Churches

John's revelations were addressed to seven churches. Jesus had messages with instructions and promises to all seven, and the words that Jesus commonly ended with to all churches were, "to him that overcometh..." These promises are listed for you in this chapter.

First, understand, we can overcome only by the blood of the Lamb (see Rev. 12:11). With that in mind, every time you read of Jesus making promises to the seven respective churches, "to him that overcometh..." I want you to think of the blood of Jesus. Also notice that just as these promises were made to the churches, so they apply to you today.

To the Church in Ephesus

...To him that overcometh will I give to eat of the tree of life, which is in the midst of the paradise of God (Revelation 2:7).

The blood is our access to the tree of life—eternal life and the life of God.

To the Church in Smyrna

...He that overcometh shall not be hurt of the second death (Revelation 2:11).

The blood prevents us from being eternally separated from God.

To the Church in Pergamos

...To him that overcometh will I give to eat of the hidden manna, and will give him a white stone, and in the stone a new name written, which no man knoweth saving he that receiveth it (Revelation 2:17).

The blood is our access to revelation knowledge.

To the Church in Thyatira

And he that overcometh, and keepeth My works unto the end, to him will I give power over the nations (Revelation 2:26).

The blood is our dominion over territories. You do not have to be afraid of territorial spirits. Just as the blood of a lamb was used in Egypt, even so the blood of Jesus prevails over any principality today.

To the Church in Sardis

He that overcometh, the same shall be clothed in white raiment; and I will not blot out His name out of the book of life, but I will confess His name before My Father, and before His angels (Revelation 3:5).

The blood is your holiness. It speaks on your behalf to the Father and decrees that the angels watch over you. It is our victory over sin.

To the Church in Philadelphia

Him that overcometh will I make a pillar in the temple of My God, and he shall go no more out: and I will write upon him the name of My God, and the name of the city of My God, which is new Jerusalem, which cometh down out of heaven from My God: and I will write upon him My new name (Revelation 3:12).

The blood is our secured foundation and strength.

To the Church in Laodicea

To him that overcometh will I grant to sit with Me in My throne, even as I also overcame, and am set down with My Father in His throne (Revelation 3:21).

The blood is our rest.

Seven Blood Impartations

> *And they sung a new song, saying, Thou art worthy to take the book, and to open the seals thereof: for Thou wast **slain**, and hast redeemed us to God by Thy blood out of every kindred, and tongue, and people, and nation; and hast made us unto our God kings and priests: and we shall reign on the earth. And I beheld, and I heard the voice of many angels round about the throne and the beasts and the elders: and the number of them was ten thousand times ten thousand, and thousands of thousands; saying with a loud voice, worthy is the Lamb that **was slain to receive power, and riches, and wisdom, and strength, and honour, and glory, and blessing*** (Revelation 5:9-12).

The word "slain" is synonymous with the shedding of blood. If they can sing about the blood in Heaven, we should certainly be singing about the blood on earth. Whatever Jesus did and achieved at Calvary, He did not do for His own benefit, but for ours. Looking at the Scriptures above, you will notice seven things that Jesus received for our benefit.

> *...worthy is the Lamb that was slain to receive power, and riches, and wisdom, and strength, and honour, and glory, and blessing* (Revelation 5:12).

Jesus received power, riches, wisdom, strength, honor, glory, and blessing! However, He did not need to go to the cross to obtain these seven blessings for Himself. He has always been more powerful than the devil. The seven blessings He received were for us.

Power

Jesus received power for us. Today you have the ability and strength of God in you. You are not a weakling or a victim. Your days of powerlessness are history. You can face life equipped with His power, for the Spirit of the living God dwells in you!

Riches

You have received riches. Jesus became poor so you can become rich. The drought is over; the curse is broken; and you do not have to be poor another day in your life. Poverty is a curse, and it is not your portion from God. God's will for your life is abundance. The apostle John reveals God's perfect will for your life:

Beloved, I wish above all things that thou mayest prosper and be in health, even as thy soul prospereth (3 John 2).

Wisdom

Jesus has been made wisdom unto you. Days of confusion and lack of direction are over. Solomon declared, *"…but **wisdom** is profitable to direct"* (Eccl. 10:10). You do not have to go through life aimless and without direction. The blood is our access to the wisdom of God from the Holy Ghost.

Strength

You are now anointed with fresh oil, and you have the strength of a wild ox because of the blood. You do not have to be a weakling anymore. Your body can remain strong. Your spirit is strong, and your mind is strong to deal with life's circumstances.

Honor

You have a crown of honor on your head. Dishonor is a thing of the past. Your days of shame are over.

Glory

God is the glory and the lifter of your head. *Glory* means to be heavily laden with good things. Because of the blood you are loaded today. You are the head and not the tail.

Blessing

Righteousness is the blessing of the New Testament. The Scripture says, *"The blessing of the Lord, it maketh rich, and He addeth no sorrow with it"* (Prov. 10:22). You can stand tall and say, "I am blessed of the Lord."

You are blessed coming in and blessed going out.

You are blessed with all spiritual blessings in heavenly places in Christ Jesus.

Victory in Jesus

O victory in Jesus, my Savior forever!

He sought me and bought me with His redeeming blood.

He loved me ere I knew Him, and all my love is due Him.

He plunged me to victory beneath the cleansing flood.

Eugene M. Bartlett

CHAPTER 6

Abel's Blood Versus Jesus' Blood

Before we delve into the contrast between Abel's blood and Jesus' blood, we need to consider why Abel's offering was satisfactory. We know that God accepted the offering of Abel while He rejected the offering of Cain. This, however, is not an implication that Cain's occupation was inferior to that of Abel.

The Problem With Cain's Offering

Why did God refuse Cain's offering but accept Abel's? Let us look at the Genesis account to gain a better understanding:

And Adam knew Eve his wife; and she conceived, and bare Cain, and said, I have gotten a man from the Lord.

And she again bare his brother Abel. And Abel was a keeper of sheep, but Cain was a tiller of the ground.

*And **in process of time** it came to pass, that Cain brought of the fruit of the ground an offering unto the Lord.*

*And Abel, he also brought of the firstlings of his flock and of the fat thereof. And the **Lord had respect unto Abel and to his offering**:*

***but unto Cain and to his offering He had not respect.** And Cain was very wroth, and his countenance fell.*

And the Lord said unto Cain, Why art thou wroth? and why is thy countenance fallen?

If thou doest well, *shalt thou not* **be accepted**? *and if thou doest not well, sin lieth at the door. And unto thee shall be his desire, and thou shalt rule over him.*

And Cain talked with Abel his brother: and it came to pass, when they were in the field, that Cain rose up against Abel his brother, and slew him.

And the Lord said unto Cain, Where is Abel thy brother? And he said, I know not: Am I my brother's keeper?

And He said, What hast thou done? the voice of thy brother's blood crieth unto Me from the ground.

And now art thou cursed from the earth, which hath opened her mouth to receive thy brother's blood from thy hand;

when thou tillest the ground, it shall not henceforth yield unto thee her strength; a fugitive and a vagabond shalt thou be in the earth (Genesis 4:1-12).

There are several words in this Scripture that are extremely important to understand. They are:

1. "In the process of time."
2. "Respect unto Abel and his offering."
3. "Doest well."
4. "Be accepted."

"In the Process of Time"

Even though the Bible does not mention ages, most scholars agree that by the time Abel and Cain gave their offering, they were fully grown men. This is where the words, "in the process of time" play an importance. In Hebrew, these words are rendered as "at the end of days," indicating a divine appointment and set time. This further reveals that this was not the first time such an offering was given and that both Cain and Abel knew and understood the importance and significance of it. The scripture records these words, "Cain brought of the fruit of the ground an offering unto the Lord. And Abel, he also brought of the firstlings of his flock and of the fat thereof...." This indicates that there was a specific time and place where offerings were presented to God. You must understand this was not something they did by chance but with full knowledge and understanding as to the reason for the offering.

There have been many debates over the years as to the cause of God's acceptance of Abel's offering and rejection of Cain's offering. One reasoning says that Abel's offering was acceptable because he offered blood. Another group rejects that belief insisting that Cain's problem was his attitude and lack of tithes. Actually, both reasons are partially right. Abel's offering was that of blood, and Cain had an attitude problem. Both Cain and Abel were sinners living outside of Eden who needed redemption. Let's get a clearer picture of this phenomenon.

"Respect Unto Abel and His Offering"

Notice these words from God: *"And the Lord had respect unto Abel and to his offering: but unto Cain and to his offering He had not respect."* The Lord respected both Abel and his offering. What is the significance of this? The key word here is "respect," which is also employed in God's dealing with His covenant people Israel:

> *And God heard their groaning, and God **remembered His covenant with Abraham, with Isaac, and with Jacob**.*
>
> *And God **looked upon** the children of Israel, and God had **respect** unto them* (Exodus 2:24-25).

I want you to see the connection between the word "covenant" and the word "respect." In light of this, you must understand that *respect* is a word used by God on the basis of covenant. Concerning Israel's deliverance, God remembered His covenant with Abraham, Isaac, and Jacob. Remember that the word *covenant* means "to cut until blood flows." He acknowledged that He was in a blood covenant with Israel. God had to acknowledge Israel because He had to acknowledge the blood covenant. God is no respecter of persons, except in the case of blood covenant.

> *For **I will have respect unto you**, and make you fruitful, and multiply you, **and establish My covenant** with you* (Leviticus 26:9).

*And the Lord was gracious unto them, and had compassion on them, and had **respect** unto them, **because of His covenant** with Abraham, Isaac, and Jacob, and would not destroy them, neither cast He them from His presence as yet* (2 Kings 13:23).

God respected Abel and his offering because a flow of blood was involved. His offering was also acceptable to God because his attitude was right. The Book of Hebrews records:

Now faith is the substance of things hoped for, the evidence of things not seen.

For by it the elders obtained a good report....

*By faith Abel offered unto God a more excellent sacrifice than Cain, **by which he obtained witness that he was righteous**, God testifying of his gifts: and by it he being dead yet speaketh* (Hebrews 11:1-2,4).

Abel offered a more excellent sacrifice by faith. Paul tells us that faith comes by hearing and hearing the Word (spoken) of God (see Rom.10:17). We see here a record of God talking to Abel and Cain as He had talked to their parents. We also know that God spoke to Cain after He rejected his offering. So in direct obedience to God's voice and instruction handed down from their parents, Abel offered the lamb. The writer of the Book of Hebrews called him "an elder" who received a good report. What was the good report? He was called "righteous." The substance of things hoped for and the evidence of things not seen was *righteousness*. The same is also said of Abraham:

For what saith the scripture? Abraham believed God, and it was counted unto him for righteousness.

Now to him that worketh is the reward not reckoned of grace, but of debt.

*But to him that worketh not, but **believeth on Him that justifieth the ungodly, his faith is counted for righteousness*** (Romans 4:3-5).

Both Abel and Abraham believed, and righteousness was imputed to them. They knew they were ungodly and there was nothing they could do to justify themselves. Abraham emphatically answered Isaac's question, *"God will provide Himself a lamb"* (Gen. 22:8a). Abraham believed in a

94

substitutionary sacrifice, and Abel also offered a substitutionary sacrifice. The lamb died in his place. You see, both Abraham and Abel believed in the future blood sacrifice of Jesus.

"If Thou Doest Well"

It is evident that Cain did not do well. His attitude was wrong, and his actions revealed he did not accept substitutionary sacrifice nor did he show faith in it. The apostle John in his Epistle tells us that Cain was of the evil one (see 1 John 3:12). Satan was behind the action of Cain. He has always wanted man to pay the price and die. His works are threefold, as revealed by Jesus when He said, *"The thief cometh not, but for to steal, and to kill, and to destroy"* (John 10:10a). Satan has always hated the idea of substitutionary blood. He wanted man's blood, and he still wants man's blood today. Cain's offering was rejected because he chose to enter God's presence his own way and not the way God had shown it should be—the way of the blood. The Epistle of Jude tells us of Cain's way, which is unacceptable to God:

Woe unto them! for they have gone in the way of Cain... (Jude 11).

The way of Cain is to enter God's presence without blood. Even the Lord Jesus did not enter the heavenly sanctuary without blood. He entered with His own blood. It is the old way, and it is the only way.

Thus saith the Lord, Stand ye in the ways, and see, and ask for the old paths, where is the good way, and walk therein, and ye shall find rest for your souls. But they said, We will not walk therein (Jeremiah 6:16).

Neither by the blood of goats and calves, but by His own blood He entered in once into the holy place, having obtained eternal redemption for us (Hebrews 9:12).

"Thou Shalt Be Accepted"

In the Bible, the word "accepted" is in connection with sacrifice and offering. If the offering was acceptable, then the person was accepted; and if the offering was unacceptable, then the person was also not accepted, as in the case of Cain. God has clearly defined in His Word, particularly in the Book of Leviticus, what is an acceptable and unacceptable offering. God told Cain he would be accepted if he did well. The acceptance would come for his offering as well as for him, if the offering was in the same form that his brother Abel had offered. Cain was not rejected because Abel was better than him; rather, it was Abel's offering that was better. The apostle John sheds some light on this issue:

> For this is the message that ye heard from the beginning, that we should love one another.
>
> Not as Cain, who was of that wicked one, and slew his brother. And wherefore slew he him? Because **his own works** were evil, and his brother's righteous (1 John 3:11-12).

John declares Cain's offering was unacceptable because it was considered "works." And from the writing of Paul, we know God does not accept works as a means of obtaining salvation.

> For by grace are ye saved through faith; and that not of yourselves: it is the gift of God: **not of works**, lest any man should boast (Ephesians 2:8-9).

Cain was aware that God had rejected the "covering works" of his father, Adam, using the fig leaves. God also rejected Cain's works; otherwise, he could have boasted in his own strength. When Cain's offering was rejected by God, he decided to kill his brother and shed his blood. God then approached Cain and told him that Abel's blood was speaking to Him from the ground.

> And Cain talked with Abel his brother: and it came to pass, when they were in the field, that Cain rose up against Abel his brother, and slew him. And the Lord said unto Cain, Where is Abel thy brother? And he said, I know not: Am I my brother's keeper? And He said, What hast thou done? **the voice of thy brother's blood crieth unto Me from the ground** (Genesis 4:8-10).

Abel's blood spoke! However, the Book of Hebrews tells us that the blood of Jesus speaks better things for us than the blood of Abel.

> And to Jesus the mediator of the new covenant, and to the blood of sprinkling, that **speaketh better things** than that of Abel (Hebrews 12:24).

I want you to notice that both the blood of Jesus and the blood of Abel spoke. For the rest of this chapter, we will look at the similarities and the differences between the two bloods. The differences will reveal why the blood of Jesus is better than the blood of Abel.

The Similarities

Both the blood of Abel and the blood of Jesus were shepherd's blood.

The Scriptures clearly state that Abel was a keeper of sheep, meaning he was a shepherd. Jesus said, *"I am the good shepherd"* (John 10:11a). In fact, the New Testament reveals Jesus as the good Shepherd, the great Shepherd, and the chief Shepherd.

The blood of both were shed by their loved ones.

Abel was killed by Cain his brother, and according to the Bible, Jesus *"came unto His own, and His own received Him not"* (John 1:11). At the Last Supper, Jesus said, *"He that dippeth his hand with Me in the dish, the same shall betray Me"* (Matt. 26:23b).

The blood of both obeyed the voice of their fathers.

The Book of Hebrews states that Abel offered a more excellent sacrifice by faith (see Heb. 11:4). We also know that Paul said to the Roman church, *"Faith cometh by hearing, and hearing…"* (Rom. 10:17). For Abel to offer an acceptable sacrifice by faith, he had to hear it from Adam who witnessed how it was done in Eden. Therefore, Abel obeyed his natural father, and Jesus, who also walked by faith (He had the testimony that He pleased God, which you have only if you are walking by faith) obeyed His heavenly Father.

The blood of both cried.

According to Genesis and Hebrews, both the blood of Jesus and the blood of Abel had a voice and spoke after they were slain.

The Differences

Abel offered a sheep in sacrifice.

> Jesus offered His own blood as sacrifice.

Abel obeyed his natural father.

> Jesus obeyed His heavenly Father.

Abel died as a sacrificer.

Jesus died as the sacrifice.

Abel's blood cried vengeance, retribution, and foul.

Jesus' blood cried victory, redemption, and forgiveness.

Abel's blood spoke from the ground (place of curse).

Jesus' blood speaks from the heavenly mercy seat.

Abel's blood manifested the curse on man.

Jesus' blood redeemed man from the curse.

Abel's shed blood was fallen human blood.

Jesus' blood is the blood of God.

Abel's blood is corruptible blood.

Jesus' blood is incorruptible blood.

Abel's blood was "sentence" blood.

Jesus' blood is saving blood.

Abel's blood was taken.

Jesus' blood was given.

Thank God that the blood of Jesus is better and speaks better things than the blood of Abel!

And Can It Be That I Should Gain?

And can it be that I should gain
An interest in the Savior's blood?
Died He for me, who caused His pain—
For me, who Him to death pursued?
Amazing love! How can it be,
That Thou, my God, shouldst die for me?
Amazing love! How can it be,
That Thou, my God, shouldst die for me?

'Tis mystery all: th'Immortal dies:
Who can explore His strange design?
In vain the firstborn seraph tries
To sound the depths of love divine.
'Tis mercy all! Let earth adore,
Let angel minds inquire no more.
'Tis mercy all! Let earth adore;
Let angel minds inquire no more.

He left His Father's throne above
So free, so infinite His grace—
Emptied Himself of all but love,
And bled for Adam's helpless race:
'Tis mercy all, immense and free,
For O my God, it found out me!
'Tis mercy all, immense and free,
For O my God, it found out me!

Charles Wesley

CHAPTER 7

Pleading the Blood

What does it mean to "plead the blood"? First of all, understand that pleading the blood has nothing to do with a beggarly mentality. It also has nothing to do with constantly repeating empty words. Many believers consider the blood as something that was shed 2,000 years ago and do not see how it can be applied to their lives in the present day. There are many today who do not believe in pleading the blood and even speak against it. They do so in ignorance. Pleading the blood is powerful and valid for today. The blood is not just for the past, but for the present as well. To plead the blood is to apply its protective power in current situations. It is to experience the power of God today.

The Blood Conquers the Powers of Darkness

And I heard a loud voice saying in heaven, Now is come salvation, and strength, and the kingdom of our God, and the power of His Christ: for the accuser of our brethren is cast down, which accused them before our God day and night. And they overcame him by the blood of the Lamb, and by the word of their testimony; and they loved not their lives unto the death (Revelation 12:10-11).

I really like the rendering of this verse from the New American Standard Version:

And they overcame him because of the blood of the Lamb and because of the word of their testimony (Revelation 12:11 NAS).

The blood of Jesus is bad news for the devil. He hates the blood of Jesus. It is his eternal defeat and destroys his hold on humanity.

It is interesting to note that the plagues of Egypt began and ended in blood. These plagues further demonstrate the effect of the blood on satan and the powers of darkness.

And the Lord spake unto Moses, Say unto Aaron, Take thy rod, and stretch out thine hand upon the waters of Egypt, upon their streams, upon their rivers, and upon their ponds, and upon all their pools of water, that they may become blood; and that there may be blood throughout all the land of Egypt, both in vessels of wood, and in vessels of stone. And Moses and Aaron did so, as the Lord commanded; and he lifted up the rod, and smote the waters that were in the river, in the sight of Pharaoh, and in the sight of his servants; and all the waters that were in the river were turned to blood. And the fish that was in the river died; and the river stank, and the Egyptians could not drink of the water of the river; and there was blood throughout all the land of Egypt (Exodus 7:18-21).

Then Moses called for all the elders of Israel, and said unto them, Draw out and take you a lamb according to your families, and kill the passover. And ye shall take a bunch of hyssop, and dip it in the blood that is in the basin, and strike the lintel and the two side posts with the blood that is in the basin; and none of you shall go out at the door of his house until the morning. For the Lord will pass through to smite the Egyptians; and when He seeth the blood upon the lintel, and on the two side posts, the Lord will pass over the door, and will not suffer the destroyer to come in unto your houses to smite you (Exodus 12:21-23).

All the plagues were sandwiched in between the blood. This was intentional, and it reveals the effect of the blood on satan. In God's mind, blood is life. To many people's way of thinking, blood symbolizes death, but as far as God is concerned, blood is a symbol of life.

For the life of the flesh is in the blood... (Leviticus 17:11).

The Blood Speaks

The blood of Jesus is the basis of our relationship with God. According to the Book of Hebrews, we are told that the blood of Jesus speaks better things for us than the blood of Abel.

*And to Jesus the mediator of the new covenant, and to the blood of sprinkling, that **speaketh better things** than that of Abel* (Hebrews 12:24).

Both the blood of Abel and Jesus were shepherd's blood, but they spoke different things. Abel's blood spoke of vengeance and judgment, whereas Jesus' blood speaks of forgiveness, justification, redemption, deliverance, healing, peace, and victory. In life, there are so many things that speak against us—the past speaks against you; your friends, family, and enemies speak against you; your sins speak against you; and satan himself, the one called "the accuser of the brethren" speaks *against* you. But thank God, we can overcome all this through the blood of Jesus, which speaks on our behalf.

Now, it is one thing for the blood to speak for us, but it is another thing to plead the blood or speak the blood. What is the difference? In the first instance, we are passive receivers, but in pleading the blood, we are actively involved.

Speaking the Blood

To plead means:

1. To argue a case in support of somebody or something, especially in a court of law.

2. To make an allegation in an action or other legal proceeding; especially to answer the previous pleading of the other party by denying facts therein stated or by alleging new facts.

3. To argue for or against a claim.

4. To maintain (as a case or cause) in a court of law or other tribunal.

5. To make intercession.

6. To contend with the adversary.

7. To speak on behalf of.

Understand that pleading the blood is not begging, but a voicing of your confidence in the blood of Jesus. Again, we want to remember to associate the words redeem and redeemed with the blood.

Many years ago, the psalmist declared, *"**Let the redeemed** of the Lord **say so**, whom He hath redeemed from the hand of the enemy"* (Ps. 107:2). It is our duty to speak forth the victory of the blood against satan. We contend with the adversary by speaking the blood. We refute his accusations by speaking the victory of the blood. Every time you speak and plead, "the blood of Jesus" you bring God's very life on the scene, and every circumstance will have to bow before you. The blood of Jesus is the all-conquering force. All things become possible through the blood. If the redemption of man, which was deemed impossible by satan, became possible, then all things are possible. I want you to hold that thought constantly in your mind. *The blood makes the impossible possible*. It will turn the battle in your favor.

The legal term "to plead" is used many times in the Old Testament. Here are a few examples and their benefits:

Pleading Keeps You From the Hands of Your Enemy and Evil

The Lord therefore be judge, and judge between me and thee, and see, and plead my cause, and deliver me out of thine hand (1 Samuel 24:15).

And when David heard that Nabal was dead, he said, Blessed be the Lord, that hath pleaded the cause of my reproach from the hand of Nabal, and hath kept His servant from evil: for the Lord hath returned the wickedness of Nabal upon his own head... (1 Samuel 25:39).

If I speak of strength, lo, he is strong: and if of judgment, who shall set me a time to plead? (Job 9:19).

Who is he that will plead with me? for now, if I hold my tongue, I shall give up the ghost (Job 13:19).

O that one might plead for a man with God, as a man pleadeth for his neighbour! (Job 16:21).

Pleading Is Victory Against Those Who Strive With You

Plead my cause, O Lord, with them that strive with me: fight against them that fight against me (Psalm 35:1).

Pleading Brings Deliverance From Deceitful and Unjust People

Judge me, O God, and plead my cause against an ungodly nation: O deliver me from the deceitful and unjust man (Psalm 43:1).

Arise, O God, plead Thine own cause: remember how the foolish man reproacheth Thee daily (Psalm 74:22).

Plead my cause, and deliver me: quicken me according to Thy word (Psalm 119:154).

Pleading Brings Restitution and Restoration

For the Lord will plead their cause, and spoil the soul of those that spoiled them (Proverbs 22:23).

For their redeemer is mighty; He shall plead their cause with thee (Proverbs 23:11).

Open thy mouth, judge righteously, and plead the cause of the poor and needy (Proverbs 31:9).

Blood's Defense in the Courtroom

In Hebrew, there are several explanations for the word *plead*, and they mean:

◆ To strive, contend.

◆ To conduct a case or suit (legal), sue.

Well, we are not suing God or striving with God—*He is not our problem*. Your problem is the devil! He is your accuser. The only effective defense is the blood of Jesus. So when we plead the blood, we are going against satan and his works. He comes against us with accusations and attacks, but when we plead the blood of Jesus, we give an expression of faith in the protective power of the blood of Jesus Christ. Remember, satan has no answer for the blood!

From the meanings of the word *plead*, we understand it is a legal term conveying the idea of a court case. Jesus, our great High Priest, is also our advocate.

> *My little children, these things write I unto you, that ye sin not. And if any man sin, we have an **advocate** with the Father, Jesus Christ the righteous* (1 John 2:1).

According to the Greek Lexicon, the word for "advocate" is *parakletos*, a legal word meaning:

- Summoned, called to one's side, especially called to one's aid.
- One who pleads another's cause before a judge, a pleader, counsel for defense, legal assistant, an advocate.
- One who pleads another's cause with one, an intercessor.

> *And I heard a loud voice saying in heaven, Now is come salvation, and strength, and the kingdom of our God, and the power of His Christ: for the accuser of our brethren is cast down, which accused them before our God day and night. And they overcame him by the blood of the Lamb, and by the word of their testimony; and they loved not their lives unto the death* (Revelation 12:10-11).

An account in the Book of Revelation gives us a picture of a court session where you have the Judge, the Defense Attorney, the accused, the witnesses, and the prosecuting attorney.

In our context, God is the Supreme Judge; Jesus is your Defense Attorney; and satan is the prosecuting attorney, or accuser, as stated in verse 10 above.

Satan's character and activities are clearly revealed in the name, "accuser of our brethren." We nullify his accusations by applying the blood. How do we do that? We plead the blood by speaking or confession! In the Old Testament, during the Exodus, the Israelites applied the blood by using the hyssop, dipping it into blood and sprinkling or smearing it upon the lintel and doorposts of the house.

> *And ye shall take a bunch of hyssop, and dip it in the blood that is in the basin, and strike the lintel and the two side posts with the blood that is in the basin; and none of you shall go out at the door of his house until the morning* (Exodus 12:22).

Well, we are not to put physical blood on our doorposts nowadays. Instead, we apply the blood today by speaking. You confess the blood just as you would the promises of God over your life. When we speak and plead the blood of Jesus, our Advocate, who is also the Apostle and High Priest of our confession, He represents us before the Father, who happens to be the Supreme Judge and negates every accusation of the enemy by virtue of His blood. Jesus calls the witnesses of His blood—the Spirit and Word—which speak for our betterment. We rest our case upon what Jesus has already provided at Calvary, and the Judge looks at us through the eyes of Christ's redemptive work. The final outcome is victory. You must understand that satan is looking for an occasion to strike at you, but the Bible says to not give him any place or foothold (see Eph. 4:27). So in prayer, which is you doing business with God, plead the protection of the blood over your life and the lives of your loved ones.

On My Way to Gosport

I remember in 1992, I was invited to minister in a church in Gosport, the south of England. Rosanna, my wife, and I were picked up by two friends early in the morning, and we started our journey. Happy to see each other, we began to talk and have fun as soon as we got in the car. I was sitting next to my friend who was driving and the girls were seated in the back. We had been traveling some miles on the expressway at about 70 miles per hour, when all of a sudden, I had this strong impression, and I said, "Hey, we did not pray as we left home. Let's pray now!" I simply said, "Lord, thank You for this trip. We plead the blood of Jesus over us and this car. Amen." I barely said, "Amen" when a semi-truck crossed over onto our lane and abruptly stopped in front of us. It was like slow motion, as my friend braked and the car tires squealed as the women screamed in the back. All I could say was, "The blood of Jesus" as I watched our car approach the back of the truck. My friend endeavored to stop the car, slamming the brakes with all his might. And just when we were about to go under the truck, somehow the car just slowed and stopped. If we had hit the back or gone under the truck, we would have been decapitated. It was the protective power of the blood of Jesus that saved us from a fatal accident.

I teach my children to plead the blood over their lives every morning. The world is full of crazy people. You have heard reports of school shootings and other horrible acts of violence. Do not take any chances with the lives of your children; take the time and draw a bloodline over them. You have nothing to lose and everything to gain. Teach them in their morning prayer time to say, "Lord, I plead the blood of Jesus over my life. I am protected by the blood. No weapon formed against me shall prosper." Teach them to say, "Devil, you cannot touch me. I am covered by the blood of Jesus, my Lord. Amen."

Saved by the Blood

Saved by the blood of the Crucified One!
Now ransomed from sin and a new work begun,
Sing praise to the Father and praise to the Son,
Saved by the blood of the Crucified One!

Glory, I'm saved! Glory, I'm saved!
My sins are all pardoned, my guilt is all gone!
Glory, I'm saved! Glory, I'm saved!
I am saved by the blood of the Crucified One!

Saved by the blood of the Crucified One!
The angels rejoicing because it is done;
A child of the Father, joint heir with the Son,
Saved by the blood of the Crucified One!

Saved by the blood of the Crucified One!
The Father He spake, and His will it was done;
Great price of my pardon, His own precious Son;
Saved by the blood of the Crucified One!

Saved by the blood of the Crucified One!
All hail to the Father, all hail to the Son,
All hail to the Spirit, the great Three in One!
Saved by the blood of the Crucified One!

S.J. Henderson

CHAPTER 8

The Covenant of Blood

If a believer wants to know more of God, it is imperative that he understand covenant, for God is a covenant-making and covenant-keeping God. Understanding covenant has been called the secret to the Bible. Without understanding covenant, the Bible would be just a religious book, and the believer would remain weak, even though all of God's resources are available to him.

We know our Bible is divided into the old and new covenants. We also understand there is a difference between them; the apostle Paul tells us the new covenant is established upon better promises. So let's have a quick look at blood covenant in this chapter before we go on and consider the tithing connection.

What Is Covenant?

A covenant is a binding agreement or obligation between two persons, tribes, or parties. It is the union of two parties to become and act as one. The strongest and most binding of covenant is the blood covenant. We see the case of binding obligation in the story of the Gibeonites, who feared for their lives after seeing what had been done to other Canaanite cities by the nation of Israel, led by Joshua. They then deceived Joshua, who cut a covenant of protection with them. The Bible says that when Joshua was deceived, he did not seek counsel from the Lord (see Josh. 9:14). And even though the Gibeonites made a covenant based upon deception and lies, Joshua was still obligated to keep it and maintain honor as he had sworn before the Lord. He had to abide by it because God does not tolerate trucebreakers.

The word *covenant* in Hebrew literally means "to cut until blood flows." As mentioned before, every time you think of the word *covenant*, you should also think of blood. The blood covenant is not an institution of man; God Himself created it in the Garden of Eden. The blood covenant between God and man began when God shed the blood of an innocent animal to cover Adam. Blood covenants have been around in almost all cultures since early civilization. The blood covenant has been the most binding, sacred agreement a person could ever enter into. *In the blood covenant, two individuals die to self and are reborn as one.* It has also been the foundation for primitive religions. We know that blood covenant has been practiced in the Middle East, parts of Asia, and certainly Africa. History has recorded some of these covenants, and the most famous to the Western mind is that of Dr. Livingstone and Dr. Stanley's expedition to Africa. From *covenant*, we also receive an important word, *friend*. A friend is a strong covenant term that refers not to just a casual acquaintance. We know that God called Abraham his friend.

Two Types of Covenants

Following are two types of covenants:

1. **Covenant of equals.**

In a covenant of equals, two strong parties merge with all their assets to gain the monopoly or dominion. A good example today is in the business realm where two major companies merge together to gain monopoly and control and thus become stronger than all other competition.

2. **Covenant of unequals.**

In a covenant of unequals, two parties unite together; however, one is stronger than the other and does not necessarily need the involvement of the weaker party. Love can be the motivation behind the covenant. A good example is God's offer to us. His union with us brought benefits to us; we had nothing to offer to God in return in terms of asset.

Reasons for the Covenant

Love, protection, and trust have been the focal reasons for cutting a covenant. The strength and reality of a covenant would promise and ensure these things and anything else the partners required. This was the foundation for faithfulness, loyalty, and dependability. The promises to the respective families would go as far as seven generations. For example, God gave many promises to Abraham and one of them was that through his seed all nations of the earth would be blessed. We see this reality in Jesus today. The reason why there are believers all over the world today is because of Jesus.

Let's look at seven reasons to enter into a covenant.

1. **Protection**.

A weaker tribe would commonly cut a covenant with a stronger tribe for the sake of protection from their enemies. The weaker tribe may not have been thrilled to enter into covenant with the stronger tribe, but the fear of being annihilated became the motivation for the covenant which then brought the protection they needed and desired.

2. **Preservation**.

The protection that the weaker party would receive from the stronger party would allow the generation of the weaker tribe to be preserved. In this way, many cultures and people have been kept and preserved for generations.

3. **Peace**.

One of the main reasons for covenant in ancient civilization was peace. At times, some of the weaker tribes would become equally strong and wealthy which caused friction, as one tribe would try to exert its superiority or prowess. Ongoing wars became very bloody; consequently, each tribe would lose many of their men in battle. Often, these battles would continue until extermination or extinction of one of the groups. Many times, due to so much death, the respective leaders of each tribe would meet to forge a covenant that would then bring peace and cessation of death in their camp.

4. *Profit*.

Two tribes would merge together to increase their profit margin. Competition between them would end, and their merge would subsequently result in the domination of other groups around them. We observe these situations in business today as well.

5. *Power*.

A covenant would also be enacted between two parties for power. In ancient civilization, survival of the fittest was the way of life. The stronger tribes would terrorize and loot the smaller tribes. However, if two tribes could be united in covenant, their strength and power were amplified.

6. *Productivity/Proliferation*.

Covenant was also cut between heads of tribes or kings promising marriage between their offspring in order to preserve or maintain the royal line through the descendants produced.

7. *Passion (Love)*.

As a seal of their love when entering marriage, a covenant was made, which symbolized two flesh becoming one soul.

Covenant Ceremonies

Although covenant ceremonies have differed in various cultures, there have been common denominators that can be connected to the blood covenant of Jesus.

The Representatives

One delegate from each party would be summoned and charged with representing each party's interest. The representative had to be someone who was qualified to speak on behalf of the tribe and to the other tribe.

Adam was our first representative, but when he sinned, he was no longer fit and acceptable to represent mankind before God.

A representative was also known as the mediator. Job verbalized his frustration of a lack of a representative or mediator.

For He is not a man, as I am, that I should answer Him, and we should come together in judgment.

Neither is there any daysman betwixt us, that might lay his hand upon us both.

Let Him take His rod away from me, and let not His fear terrify me: then would I speak, and not fear Him; but it is not so with me (Job 9:32-35).

For He is not a man like me, that I can answer Him,

that we can take each other to court. There is no one to judge between us,

to lay his hand on both of us (Job 9:32-33 HCSB).

God and I are not equals; I can't bring a case against Him. We'll never enter a courtroom as peers. How I wish we had an arbitrator to step in and let me get on with life... (Job 9:32-33 MSG).

A "daysman," as stated in the King James Version, was a mediator. Job's perception was that he needed somebody suitable and qualified to represent him to God, but he found none, which brought great despair to him. Then it was revealed to him that a Mediator was coming.

Oh that my words were now written! Oh that they were printed in a book!

That they were graven with an iron pen and lead in the rock for ever!

For I know that my Redeemer liveth, and that He shall stand at the latter day upon the earth (Job 19:23-25).

But I know there is someone in heaven who will come at last to my defense

even after my skin is eaten by disease, while still in this body I will see God. I will see him with my own eyes, and he will not be a stranger... (Job 19:25-27 GNB).

Now Jesus is known as the Mediator:

*For there is one God, and **one mediator** between God and men, the man Christ Jesus* (1 Timothy 2:5).

*But now hath He obtained a more excellent ministry, by how much also **He is the mediator** of a better covenant, which was established upon better promises* (Hebrews 8:6).

Jesus was the perfect man, the righteous man, who could legally represent and mediate for us to God. Job boldly declared, "I have found my Mediator, my Representative, He is my Redeemer. He is in Heaven, He lives and He will come to earth." Job testified of the Redeemer's preexistence even before He came to earth, and he also called Him God. Jesus Christ is not some mere man; He is God, and He came to earth as the God-Man to properly represent and redeem mankind.

Garment Exchange

What was the point of exchanging garments, belts, and weapons when making a covenant? In First Samuel 18, Jonathan made a covenant with David where the Bible says he became one in spirit with David because he loved him as himself.

And Jonathan stripped himself of the robe that was upon him, and gave it to David, and his garments, even to his sword, and to his bow, and to his girdle (1 Samuel 18:4).

The clothing represented the identity and authority of the person, and each partner took on the identity of the other in an exchange of that clothing. David put on Jonathan's kingly robe, and Jonathan put on David's shepherd's outfit. The belt that was worn carried the sword and dagger representing strength. Each partner would promise to make his strength fully available to the other. The weapons also represented protection. A covenant partner would lay his sword at the feet of the other as a sign of his vow to protect his covenant friend until death. In the exchanging of weapons, each was saying, "If anyone attacks you, they are attacking me, for we are one." All assets and all debts were merged as two became one.

How does that apply to us today?

Jesus, our Covenant Partner and Mediator, has given us His armor and His weapons. He has sworn to protect us. He has also declared that He will never leave us nor forsake us. He is our shield and buckler, and we can abide under the shadow of the Almighty.

The Blood Sacrifice

Looking at the covenant ceremony between God and Abraham, you will discover that five animals were sacrificed. In the Scriptures the number *five* is connected to grace.

And He said unto him, I am the Lord that brought thee out of Ur of the Chaldees, to give thee this land to inherit it.

And he said, Lord God, whereby shall I know that I shall inherit it?

*And He said unto him, **Take Me an heifer of three years old, and a she goat of three years old, and a ram of three years old, and a turtledove, and a young pigeon**.*

*And **he took unto Him all these, and divided them in the midst, and laid each piece one against another**: but the birds divided he not.*

And when the fowls came down upon the carcases, Abram drove them away.

And when the sun was going down, a deep sleep fell upon Abram; and, lo, an horror of great darkness fell upon him.

And He said unto Abram, Know of a surety that thy seed shall be a stranger in a land that is not theirs, and shall serve them; and they shall afflict them four hundred years;

and also that nation, whom they shall serve, will I judge: and afterward shall they come out with great substance.

And thou shalt go to thy fathers in peace; thou shalt be buried in a good old age (Genesis 15:7-15).

Typically, in a blood covenant ceremony, the animals were cut straight down the backbone and placed side by side with a river of blood flowing between. Today in our modern society, the red carpet that is used in a wedding ceremony is symbolic of the river of blood with the representatives of each party standing on opposite sides. The cutting of the animals in two equal halves reveals to us that the two representatives are becoming one. The two halves of the animals, equally split, were originally one.

The Blood Path

And it came to pass, that, when the sun went down, and it was dark, behold a smoking furnace, and a burning lamp that passed between those pieces.

In the same day the Lord made a covenant with Abram, saying, Unto thy seed have I given this land, from the river of Egypt unto the great river, the river Euphrates (Genesis 15:17-18).

The covenant partners or representatives would then join their hands and walk twice through and around the halves of the dead animal in a figure eight which spoke of infinity.

When God was cutting the covenant, we know that Abraham was sound asleep. *"And when the sun was going down, a deep sleep fell upon Abram…"* (Gen. 15:12). During the ceremony of the bloodpath, a "smoking furnace," meaning God, and the "burning lamp," meaning Christ Jesus walked together through the pieces. The surety of the covenant was between God and Jesus. God knew that mere man would fail, but Jesus our Mediator, the God-Man, our substitute, would not fail us.

The Mingling of Blood

According to the writing of Moses, *"The life of the flesh is in the blood"* (Lev. 17:11). Advertisements today encourage people to give blood in order to help someone else live. The giving of blood represents the giving of life, and the taking of blood is the taking of life. We can give blood, but we are forbidden to take away life or drink of blood. The mixing and mingling of the two bloods means they receive each other's life. This is how two unrelated people become one "flesh and blood."

There were several ways for mingling blood:

1. The now-covenant partners would simply stand in the river of warm blood from the sacrificed animal, which acted as their substitution.

2. The now-covenant partners would stand in the river of warm blood from the sacrificed animal, make an incision in their hand, and mingle their blood.

3. In certain cultures, after a cut was made in the palms of the two representatives, drops of each representative's blood would be caught and mingled in a cup of wine from which each would drink. God strictly forbade this:

    Every moving thing that liveth shall be meat for you; even as the green herb have I given you all things.

    But flesh with the life thereof, which is the blood thereof, shall ye not eat (Genesis 9:3-4).

Whatsoever soul it be that eateth any manner of blood, even that soul shall be cut off from his people (Leviticus 7:27).

And whatsoever man there be of the house of Israel, or of the strangers that sojourn among you, that eateth any manner of blood; I will even set my face against that soul that eateth blood, and will cut him off from among his people (Leviticus 17:10).

4. The two covenant representatives would make an incision in the palms of their hands and then grip them together to mingle the blood. This is where the handshake originated.

5. A cut would be made in both covenant partners' right wrists, which would then be held up high while gripping each other's hand; the blood would flow and mingle down their arms.

6. There was also a belief that the left ring finger connected directly to the heart. A cut around that finger was made, drawing blood. Black powder would then be rubbed into the cut to create a visible marked scar when healed. This would make a ring that could never be pulled off. Everyone who saw it would automatically know that that person had made a covenant. Later in history, a gold ring was worn as a substitute, marking the origin of the wedding ring. When Jesus showed Thomas His hands and told him to put his hand in them, on those hands was the scar of the covenant. Jesus, our Covenant Partner has nail-scarred hands and feet.

The Sworn Oaths, the Blessings, and the Curses

The partners would then swear to each other in a solemn oath. Once the oath was taken, the covenant was sealed and established. It was the point of no return. It could never be broken, as to do so would incur curses. Once the oath was confirmed and one party willingly broke the agreement, he would be marked for death.

Brethren, I speak after the manner of men; Though it be but a man's covenant, yet if it be confirmed, no man disannulleth, or addeth thereto (Galatians 3:15).

For when God made promise to Abraham, because He could swear by no greater, He sware by Himself,

Saying, Surely blessing I will bless thee, and multiplying I will multiply thee.

And so, after he had patiently endured, he obtained the promise.

For men verily swear by the greater: and an oath for confirmation is to them an end of all strife.

Wherein God, willing more abundantly to show unto the heirs of promise the immutability of His counsel, confirmed it by an oath:

that by two immutable things, in which it was impossible for God to lie, we might have a strong consolation, who have fled for refuge to lay hold upon the hope set before us (Hebrew 6:13-18).

With the oath, the terms of the covenant and the blessings that would follow were stated. Now the amazing thing is that God Himself took an oath. He has never broken His Word! His Word alone would have been sufficient. So why the oath? It was not for His benefit that He kept His Word. He was going to do that anyway. Rather, the oath was for the benefit of Abraham and for us.

I call heaven and earth to record this day against you, that I have set before you life and death, blessing and cursing: therefore choose life, that both thou and thy seed may live (Deuteronomy 30:19).

Change of Names

The covenant partners would exchange or join their names at the time of the covenant ceremony. Each party would add his covenant partner's name to his, or one might take the other's name as is still common in marriage today. Abram was no longer just Abram, but Abraham, and Sarai, his wife's name, was changed to Sarah. The "H" was added as it came from God's name, Jehovah, Abraham's covenant friend. God also became known as the God of Abraham, Isaac, and Jacob. The exchange of names also gave each party the power of attorney.

Covenant Meal

One of the most important aspects of the covenant ceremony was the meal. They would break bread and drink wine. Bread represents flesh, and wine represents blood and spirit. The covenant partners would break the bread in half and feed the pieces to one another, signifying the joining of their flesh. Wine also symbolized joy to the Hebrews. The meal symbolized

120

the joining of life, blood, and spirit. Each symbolically said, "My body is your body; my blood is your blood." The two became one—in thought, action, and voice. In addition to bread and wine, the sacrificial animal would have been cooked and eaten at the covenant meal.

Jesus did this very same thing in what is commonly known as the Last Supper.

And as they were eating, Jesus took bread, and blessed it, and brake it, and gave it to the disciples, and said, Take, eat; this is My body.

And He took the cup, and gave thanks, and gave it to them, saying, Drink ye all of it; for this is My blood of the new testament, which is shed for many for the remission of sins.

But I say unto you, I will not drink henceforth of this fruit of the vine, until that day when I drink it new with you in My Father's kingdom.

And when they had sung an hymn, they went out into the mount of Olives (Matthew 26:26-30).

The bread that He broke represented His own body and the wine which they drank represented His blood or life.

The Memorial, Witness, or Sign

The memorial served as a reminder to all parties of the solemn agreement that had been made. In most cases, a tree would be planted; otherwise, a heap of stones was erected.

For example, Abraham and Abimelech planted a memorial tree.

Thus they made a covenant at Beersheba: then Abimelech rose up, and Phichol the chief captain of his host, and they returned into the land of the Philistines. And Abraham planted a grove in Beersheba, and called there on the name of the Lord, the everlasting God (Genesis 21:32-33).

Abraham planted a tree as witness to the covenant he made with Abimelech. The tree also represented the strength of the covenant as it would increase and grow larger. Of course, we know that Jesus hung on a tree for us—the cross. It is a memorial that will stand forever. The apostle Paul declared that he preached the cross.

121

Another example, Jacob and Laban erected a stone pillar as witness to their covenant. The pillar would serve as a constant reminder to keep the oath.

Now therefore come thou, let us make a covenant, I and thou; and let it be for a witness between me and thee. And

Jacob took a stone, and set it up for a pillar. And

Jacob said unto his brothers, Gather stones; and they took stones, and made an heap: and they did eat there upon the heap. And

Laban called it Jegar-sahadutha: but Jacob called it Galeed. And

Laban said, This heap is a witness between me and thee this day. Therefore was the name of it called Galeed;

and Mizpah; for he said, The Lord watch between me and thee, when we are absent one from another.

If thou shalt afflict my daughters, and if thou shalt take other wives beside my daughters, no man is with us; see, God is witness betwixt me and thee. And

Laban said to Jacob, Behold this heap, and behold this pillar, which I have cast betwixt me and thee;

this heap be witness, and this pillar be witness, that I will not pass over this heap to thee, and that thou shalt not pass over this heap and this pillar unto me, for harm.

The God of Abraham, and the God of Nahor, the God of their father, judge betwixt us. And Jacob sware by the fear of his father Isaac. Then

Jacob offered sacrifice upon the mount, and called his brethren to eat bread: and they did eat bread, and tarried all night in the mount. And early in the morning Laban rose up, and kissed his sons and his daughters, and blessed them: and Laban departed, and returned unto his place (Genesis 31:44-55).

Our memorial was and is the tree of Calvary.

CHAPTER 9

The Promises Through the Blood to Abraham's Seed

Paul boldly declares to us in his Galatians Epistle, *"If ye be Christ's, then are ye Abraham's seed, and heirs according to the promise"* (Gal. 3:29). What does that mean for you today? How does it affect your life? You know that you belong to Christ because He paid the price for you as Paul reminded the church in Corinth. However, this means more than a change of owners; there are also privileges attached. As a seed of Abraham, you are an heir. This means that you have an inheritance. Don't fret if your parents have died and didn't leave you anything in their will. What you now possess as a seed of Abraham is beyond your wildest imagination.

> *Christ hath redeemed us from the curse of the law, being made a curse for us: for it is written, Cursed is every one that hangeth on a tree:* **that the blessing of Abraham** *might come on the Gentiles through Jesus Christ...* (Galatians 3:13-14).

> *Now to Abraham and his seed were the promises made* (Galatians 3:16a).

The "blessing of Abraham" and the "promises made" to Abraham are two distinct entities. "Blessing" is singular, while "promises," plural, suggest many. The blessing of Abraham is righteousness by faith.

> *For what saith the scripture? Abraham believed God, and it was counted unto him for righteousness. Now to him that worketh is the reward not reckoned of grace, but of debt. But to him that*

worketh not, but believeth on Him that justifieth the ungodly, his faith is counted for righteousness. Even as David also describeth the blessedness of the man, unto whom God imputeth righteousness without works, saying, Blessed are they whose iniquities are forgiven, and whose sins are covered. Blessed is the man to whom the Lord will not impute sin....

For the promise, that he should be the heir of the world, was not to Abraham, or to his seed, through the law, but through the righteousness of faith (Romans 4:3-8,13).

Just as God imputed righteousness to Abraham because of his faith, we receive the blessing of righteousness by faith too. Righteousness is the greatest blessing of the new covenant because it is the nature of God invested into your spirit man. Righteousness is defined as the ability to go before a holy God without the sense of sin or inferiority complex. It is right standing with God. Solomon says,

The blessing of the Lord, *it maketh rich, and He addeth no sorrow with it* (Proverbs 10:22).

Notice, it is the blessing that brings you to a wealthy place. In other words, we could not partake of the promises and goodness of God unless we had the blessing of righteousness deposited into our lives. The promises come with the blessing. Now what are the promises that God made to Abraham and his seed?

The Promises to Abraham and His Seed

Now the Lord had said unto Abram, Get thee out of thy country, and from thy kindred, and from thy father's house, unto a land that I will show thee: and I will make of thee a great nation, and I will bless thee, and make thy name great; and thou shalt be a blessing: and I will bless them that bless thee, and curse him that curseth thee: and in thee shall all families of the earth be blessed (Genesis 12:1-3).

The promises of God are:

- ◆ I will show you a land.
- ◆ I will make you a great nation.
- ◆ I will bless you.

- I will make your name great.

- You will be a blessing.

- In you will all the families of the earth be blessed.

- I will bless those who bless you.

- I will curse those who curse you.

These promises do not only belong to the physical seed of Abraham but also to you because you are a seed of Abraham today. These promises apply as much to you as they do to Israel. They are yours because of blood redemption.

I Will Show You a Land

"The earth is the Lord's and the fulness thereof" (Ps. 24:1a). Even as Israel has a legal right to their homeland, whether others like it or not, you also have a right to land. Was it not said that Joseph became the lord of the land or the landlord? The same will be said about you. Every believer has a God-given right to have his or her own land and property. That is your covenant promise from God.

I Will Make You a Great Nation

When Abraham and Sarah came to God, they had no children. In fact, Sarah was barren, and Abraham was an old man. The Book of Deuteronomy states that barrenness is a curse, but covenant will reverse this curse. The purpose of covenant is fruitfulness. As covenant partners of God, you will be fruitful and have blessed and mighty children. A great nation is not one who is on drugs, running away from God and wild. As covenant partners, claim that your children are great and increasing in wisdom and stature.

I Will Bless You

When Abraham first came to God, he was not blessed. According to the Amplified Bible, the word *blessed* means "happy, prosperous, and to be envied." But before Abraham came to God, no one envied him. He had no heir, no money, and a barren wife. How his life changed when he cut a covenant with God! To be blessed also means to empower, to prosper, and to receive an impartation of blessings.

In effect, God said to Abraham, "Whatever failed in your life before, I will empower to prosper." The same applies to you today! Whatever failed yesterday, God will make it work today. How did God bless Abraham? When you discover what blessings God gave to Abraham, then you will also know what is available for you.

And Abram was very rich in cattle, in silver, and in gold (Genesis 13:2).

How did he obtain the silver and gold? When he had left Haran earlier, he didn't have any silver or gold. So who gave it to him? Eliezar, Abraham's servant, sheds some light on this subject:

And he said, I am Abraham's servant. And the Lord hath blessed my master greatly; and he is become great: and He hath given him flocks, and herds, and silver, and gold, and menservants, and maidservants, and camels, and asses (Genesis 24:34-35).

God gave the silver and gold to Abraham as well as servants, camels, and donkeys. The reason why God could give them to Abraham is because the silver and gold of this earth are His. He owns all the cattle on a thousand hills. Because Abraham is His covenant partner and covenant implies two becoming one, whatever belonged to God was also Abraham's property. You are Abraham's seed; therefore, you also have right to silver and gold. You do not have to be poor when your Partner is the Owner of Heaven and earth.

I Will Make Your Name Great

Every believer can be a person of influence. Your name speaks of who you are. In the world, people make their name great by what they achieve. As a child of God, you are marked for greatness. You are to be a high achiever-believer! When Abram came to God, his name was not great until God inserted part of His name into Abram's name, calling him Abraham. God's name in his name made Abraham great. Today you have the name of Jesus because of the blood covenant that we have with God. In fact, this name is now the believer's inheritance. The name of Jesus is above every name according to the Scriptures (see Phil. 2). Therefore, you as a believer have a right to be a person of influence because you are connected to Him. Your name will become great in your city and your workplace.

You Will Be a Blessing

God will bless you so much that you will have plenty left over to meet the needs of others. That is the highest walk in life! God never meant for you to barely get by. Your God's name is El Shaddai, not "El Get-by." As He takes you into your wealthy place, you will become a point of blessings for others. You will empower others. But you cannot empower others if you are not first empowered. You cannot be a blessing to others if you are not blessed. Therefore, to be a blessing, you will be blessed.

"Well, Brother Glenn, I don't want much—just enough for me and my family." That does not sound like you want to be a blessing. If you want to be a blessing, then get ready for the more abundant life. Get ready to move from a place of not enough to a place of more than enough. Get ready for more money so you can bless the work of God, your church, and those who have needs around you. To be a blessing also means you will have a generous spirit, just as God has a generous spirit. Paul tells us that we have been blessed with all blessings—a reality because of the blood of Jesus. You have everything so that you can become a blessing to everyone else.

In You Will All the Families of the Earth Be Blessed

God has more on His mind than just the needs of you and your family. Thank God that He blesses us because He has the world on His mind. He wants to bless the world and to bring happiness to those in it. Thank God you can be a blessing to the world and not just your neighbor. Do you realize that the Internet is a blessing to the world? One idea has changed and facilitated the way we communicate, and we can access information from the comfort of our home. God wants to give you the ideas for witty and useful inventions as well so that the world can be blessed by you. Believe God for it. The next new wave of modern technology advances can come through you.

I Will Bless Those Who Bless You

What a promise from God! To bless means to empower, to prosper, to promote, and to do good to. God is saying that He will make sure that whoever causes you to go forward will go forward as well. God, as your Covenant Partner, will bless, promote, and give good things to whoever does a good thing for you in order to lift you up or promote you. Your friend will become His friend.

I Will Curse Those Who Curse You

To curse means to empower to fail, to demote, or to go against. God, your blood Covenant Partner, says that if someone is foolish enough to go against you, to try to do evil against you and cause you to fail, He will take it personally and will arrange their demise. Your enemies are in trouble because they have also become the enemies of your Covenant Partner. I never worry about witches and warlocks who try to do me harm, for I know it will backfire against them. God will demote whoever tries to demote me. My God will arrange the failure of whoever tries to cause me to fail. You see, I have faith in what God has said about me as a seed of Abraham. I believe that no weapon formed against me in any way or form can prosper.

Now you understand why God had to move against Egypt the way He did. It was not because God did not like Egyptians. In fact, He blessed Egypt because of Joseph. God loves everybody; however, when you touch His blood covenant people, you face the consequences, irrespective of your race, nationality, or color.

The Bible talks of two pharaohs—one who blessed, released, and promoted Joseph from the pit to the palace, and the other pharaoh who did not know of Joseph and who dared to raise his hands against God's people. How did God respond to each of these leaders? To the one who promoted Joseph, God protected his nation from the seven years of severe famine and caused them to prosper through it. Why? Because this pharaoh did good to Abraham's seed. As he protected Joseph, so God protected him. As he promoted Joseph, so God promoted him.

What of the other ignorant pharaoh who did not know Joseph and then afflicted the Israelites?

Now there arose up a new king over Egypt, which knew not Joseph.

And he said unto his people, Behold, the people of the children of Israel are more and mightier than we: Come on, let us deal wisely with them; lest they multiply, and it come to pass, that, when there falleth out any war, they join also unto our enemies, and fight against us, and so get them up out of the land.

Therefore they did set over them taskmasters to afflict them with their burdens. *And they built for Pharaoh treasure cities, Pithom and Raamses.*

But the more they afflicted them, the more they multiplied and grew. And they were grieved because of the children of Israel.

And the Egyptians made the children of Israel to serve with rigour:

and they made their lives bitter with hard bondage, in mortar, and in brick, and in all manner of service in the field: all their service, wherein they made them serve, was with rigour (Exodus 1:8-14).

He increased their pain and was stubborn against them. Consequently, God had no choice but to move against Egypt. If God had ignored their predicament and not reacted, He would have broken His covenant and been deemed a liar. God had to cause Egypt to fail, and the nation did. After all the plagues, Egypt was left in ruin and abject shame. Previously, the children of Israel had worked hard as slaves without pay, so when it was time to leave, God made sure the Israelites received their rightful income from the Egyptians. I want you to understand that because the pharaoh and Egypt dared to raise their hands against the blood covenant friends and partners of God, He was left with no choice but to destroy Egypt. The Bible also declares that whoever shall rise against you shall fall. I love what the prophet Isaiah said many years ago:

*Behold, they shall surely gather together, but not by Me: **whosoever** shall gather together against thee shall fall for thy sake* (Isaiah 54:15).

Notice the word "whosoever," referring to those who come against you. Now he may call himself "boss" or "president," but God calls him a "whosoever"; and why should you be afraid of a "whosoever" when the Greater One dwells in you? When you understand that you are Abraham's seed, there will be an air of confidence in you and a spring in your step because:

No weapon that is formed against thee shall prosper; and every tongue that shall rise against thee in judgment thou shalt condemn. This is the heritage of the servants of the Lord, and their righteousness is of Me, saith the Lord (Isaiah 54:17).

The Promise of Exceeding Great Reward

> After these things the word of the Lord came unto Abram in a vision, saying, Fear not, Abram: **I am thy shield, and thy exceeding great reward** (Genesis 15:1).

This event and promise occurred immediately after Abraham gave his tithes to Melchizedek, the priest of the Most High God. God said to Abraham, "I am your shield," meaning, "I am your protector." No harm would come to him. Then He said, "I am your exceeding great reward." The following three words will change your life.

- *Exceeding*, meaning "quick and speedy."

- *Great*, meaning "increase and multiply."

- *Reward*, meaning "wages, passage money, or money supply."

When you combine these three words, they become "speedy increase of money supply." God gave a promise to Abraham, and because you are Abraham's seed, He says to you as well, "I am your quick multiplication of wages." Get ready for your life to change. God wants to increase your salary.

The Promise of El Shaddai

> And when Abram was ninety years old and nine, the Lord appeared to Abram, and said unto him, I am the Almighty God; walk before Me, and be thou perfect.
>
> And I will make My covenant between Me and thee, and will multiply thee exceedingly (Genesis 17:1-2).

When Abraham was 99 years old, his body had become impotent. The Bible says that he was as good as dead. But God revealed Himself to Abraham as Almighty God. In the Hebrew, His name is El Shaddai.

What does *El Shaddai* mean?

Many have said that it means the "Breasty One" or the "All Sufficient God." The King James Version translates it as "Almighty God." He is supreme, sovereign, with absolute power. As great as this sounds, yet it still does not do justice to this great name of God.

El Shaddai is a combination of two Hebrew words—*El* and *Shaddai*. From the word *El*, we also get the word *Elohim*, which literally means strong and mighty and refers to God in His creative ability. It is God in His sovereign, governing, and creative power who creates and sets things to move in a certain way and fashion. In the first chapter of Genesis, we see God as *Elohim* who creates nature to flow in a certain way. He sets the sunrise and the sunset, the moon to rule by night, and the sun to rule by day. Once He sets those things, no one can tamper with them. In a simplistic way, *Elohim* refers to God who creates nature.

Shaddai is connected to the word "breast," indicating that which feeds, nourishes, nurtures, provides, and satisfies. When you connect the word *Shaddai* to the word *El*, it then translates to "the One who nourishes, nurtures, and satisfies." It also means the "Shedder of blessings." You have to remember that God gave this promise to Abraham when his body as well as his wife's body could not bring forth a child. *Shaddai* also means "violently reverse or accelerate." God said to Abraham, "Nature says that you are old as is your wife, and nothing you two could ever do will bring forth a baby. Nature and time are against you. But as El Shaddai, I reserve the right to undo what nature and time has done to you. I can reverse any curse and accelerate any blessings in your life."

This is good news! God can and will change anything that needs reversed in your life. You are Abraham's seed and you qualify. God will turn back the clock for you. You are not beyond your miracle. Can you see how the blood has a tremendous impact upon the lives of God's covenant people?

All these precious promises also apply to you. God only wants you to hook your faith to His promises, and they will be unleashed in your life so that He can take you to a higher level of existence.

CHAPTER 10

Tithes and the Blood

And when Abram heard that his brother was taken captive, he armed his trained servants, born in his own house, three hundred and eighteen, and pursued them unto Dan.

And he divided himself against them, he and his servants, by night, and smote them, and pursued them unto Hobah, which is on the left hand of Damascus.

And he brought back all the goods, and also brought again his brother Lot, and his goods, and the women also, and the people.

And the king of Sodom went out to meet him after his return from the slaughter of Chedorlaomer, and of the kings that were with him, at the valley of Shaveh, which is the king's dale.

And Melchizedek king of Salem brought forth bread and wine: and he was the priest of the most high God.

And he blessed him, and said, Blessed be Abram of the most high God, possessor of heaven and earth: and blessed be the most high God, which hath delivered thine enemies into thy hand. And he gave him tithes of all.

And the king of Sodom said unto Abram, Give me the persons, and take the goods to thyself.

And Abram said to the king of Sodom, I have lift up mine hand unto the Lord, the most high God, the possessor of heaven and earth, that I will not take from a thread even to a shoelatchet, and that I will not take any thing that is thine, lest thou shouldest say, I have made Abram rich (Genesis 14:14-23).

Melchizedek, in the Old Testament, was a type of the Lord Jesus. He was the king of Salem, which meant king of peace, and he was also the priest of the Most High God. Paul, in his Epistle tells us that Jesus is a priest *"after the order of Melchizedek"* (Heb. 7:11).

I want you to notice that Melchizedek brought bread and wine; subsequently, Abraham brought his tithes. Bread and wine reminds us of the Lord's table. The wine represents His blood, and the bread His body. Notice that it was Melchizedek who came first with the bread and wine. The same applies to us. Jesus our High Priest is the One who came to meet with man. Just as Melchizedek brought bread and wine, Jesus brought and gave us His body and blood. Melchizedek then blessed Abraham, who then in turn, gave his tithes. Jesus has blessed us with His shed blood and body. Abraham connected with his priest through the tithes, and we connect with our covenant through our tithes.

Tithing is for today. Tithes are your covenant connection. The covenant has already been cut, and blood has flowed; and you remain under the protection or covering through the tithes. God does not allow the destroyer to harm those who stay in touch under the cover of the blood, and He will not allow the devourer to eat or destroy the fruit of your ground. There are blessings and protection through tithing. Consider the benefits of tithing as follows:

Will a man rob God? Yet ye have robbed Me. But ye say, Wherein have we robbed Thee? In tithes and offerings.

Ye are cursed with a curse: for ye have robbed Me, even this whole nation.

Bring ye all the tithes into the storehouse, that there may be meat in Mine house, and prove Me now herewith, saith the Lord of hosts, if I will not open you the windows of heaven, and pour you out a blessing, that there shall not be room enough to receive it.

And I will rebuke the devourer for your sakes, and he shall not destroy the fruits of your ground; neither shall your vine cast her fruit before the time in the field, saith the Lord of hosts.

And all nations shall call you blessed: for ye shall be a delightsome land, saith the Lord of hosts (Malachi 3:8-12).

1. God will rebuke the devourer for your sake.
2. Tithing will enlarge and increase your income.
3. God will open the windows of Heaven for you.
4. You can prove God with your tithes.
5. You won't have room to contain all your blessings through tithing.
6. Nations will call you blessed.
7. You will be a delightsome land.

CHAPTER 11

The Salvation of Your Loved Ones Through the Blood

Your loved ones can be saved!

A lot of people have given up praying for their loved ones to be saved because they constantly see the rebellion and animosity of their loved ones towards the Gospel. They feel their relatives are a lost cause and have resigned to losing their family to hell.

The devil wants you to feel despondent and lose all hope. He will whisper in your mind, "Look at your husband! He will never get saved. He hates you and your God. Do you remember how you had harmony in your house before you started testifying to him? Leave him alone and you can have harmony once again."

Let me remind you—the devil is a liar!

Your husband will be saved.

Your daughter will be saved.

Your son will be saved.

Your loved one will be saved.

You may say, "Oh Brother Glenn, you don't know my husband!"

I don't need to. I know Jesus and His Word. He cannot lie. Rather, He has given us His precious promises concerning your family's salvation in His Word. You have to believe that God wants your loved one saved.

Does God Want Everyone to Be Saved?

To start, let's destroy the erroneous idea that God wants some people saved but not others—in which case, no matter what a person does, he cannot be saved because God, in His infinite wisdom and sovereignty, did not choose Him. Is that the Gospel of Jesus Christ? No, a thousand times no! That is a despicable lie from the pit. God wants all men saved! That is His will. How do I know that? The Word is the revelation of the will of God. The Bible is the place to start if you want to find the will of God. Let's look at the testimonies of the two most important persons in the New Testament:

Jesus' Testimony

For the Son of man is come to seek and to save that which was lost (Luke 19:10).

For God so loved the world, that He gave His only begotten Son, that whosoever believeth in Him should not perish, but have everlasting life.

For God sent not His Son into the world to condemn the world; but that the world through Him might be saved (John 3:16-17).

We all know that Jesus cannot lie; in Him is the truth. In fact, He is the truth. Jesus said He was sent to save the world; that means everybody has the right to be saved according to Jesus.

Paul's Testimony

*I exhort therefore, that, first of all, supplications, prayers, intercessions, and giving of thanks, be made **for all men**; for kings, and for all that are in authority; that we may lead a quiet and peaceable life in all godliness and honesty.*

For this is good and acceptable in the sight of God our Saviour;

*who **will have all men to be saved**, and to come unto the knowledge of the truth.*

For there is one God, and one mediator between God and men, the man Christ Jesus; who gave Himself a ransom for all, to be testified in due time (1 Timothy 2:1-6).

For the grace of God that bringeth salvation hath appeared to all men (Titus 2:11).

The apostle Paul emphatically reveals the will of God for all men to be saved. He even encourages prayers for men to be saved. Both Jesus and Paul agree that all men can be saved. Jesus died and was raised to save the vilest sinner. Get that into your spirit. Settle it once and for all. God wants to save your loved ones.

He wants to save your husband.

He wants to save your wife.

He wants to save your son and daughter.

A Promise for Your Family

There is a tremendous promise in the Book of Acts that I want to draw your attention to:

And brought them out, and said, Sirs, what must I do to be saved?

And they said, Believe on the Lord Jesus Christ, and thou shalt be saved, and thy house (Acts 16:30-31).

Pay special attention to the words spoken to the Philippian jailer, *"...thou shalt be saved, and thy house."* What a great promise! The word "house" in Greek also means "family." This verse can be translated as, "You shall be saved and your family." There you have it! Your house or your family has a God-given right to be saved.

Do we have more examples in the Bible? Yes, we do. The Scriptures say, *"In the mouth of two or three witnesses every word may be established"* (Matt. 18:16). Apart from the jailer in the Book of Acts, I want to give you six examples of God saving an entire family so that you can increase your faith and confidence for your family. Remember, God is no respecter of persons. He has saved families in the past; He is faithful and He will do so for you.

Noah

We all have heard of the great patriarch Noah who built the ark. In this account, you will see that his house was saved and missed the judgment of the flood.

*And the Lord said unto Noah, **Come thou and all thy house** into the ark; for thee have I seen righteous before Me in this generation....*

And Noah did according unto all that the Lord commanded him....

And Noah went in, and his sons, and his wife, and his sons' wives with him, into the ark, because of the waters of the flood (Genesis 7:1,5,7).

God did not just save Noah from the flood, but his wife, his sons, and their wives as well.

Israel

The night that the death angel destroyed all the firstborn of Egypt, the Lord gave a promise to Moses:

For I will pass through the land of Egypt this night, and will smite all the firstborn in the land of Egypt, both man and beast; and against all the gods of Egypt I will execute judgment: I am the Lord.

And the blood shall be to you for a token upon the houses where ye are: and when I see the blood, I will pass over you, and the plague shall not be upon you to destroy you, when I smite the land of Egypt....

And ye shall take a bunch of hyssop, and dip it in the blood that is in the basin, and strike the lintel and the two side posts with the blood that is in the basin; and none of you shall go out at the door of his house until the morning.

For the Lord will pass through to smite the Egyptians; and when he seeth the blood upon the lintel, and on the two side posts, the Lord will pass over the door, and will not suffer the destroyer to come in unto your houses to smite you (Exodus 12:12-13,22-23).

As many as were in the house that night were saved and kept from the destroyer. It did not matter whether they were old or young, male or female—as long as they were in the house they were saved.

Rahab

Salvation visited the house of the harlot who hid the two spies of Joshua. All of Jericho was facing judgment. The city would soon fall and destruction was imminent, yet Rahab and her household were saved.

And the city shall be accursed, even it, and all that are therein, to the Lord: **only Rahab the harlot shall live, she and all that are with her in the house**, *because she hid the messengers that we sent* (Joshua 6:17).

And Joshua saved Rahab the harlot alive, and her father's household, and all that she had; *and she dwelleth in Israel even unto this day; because she hid the messengers, which Joshua sent to spy out Jericho* (Joshua 6:25).

Cornelius

Church history tells us this was the first time revival came to the Gentiles. The Roman centurion was a candidate for breakthrough as well as his family. Prior to Peter's arrival, he did not know the way of salvation, but when it came, his whole house experienced it.

*There was a certain man in Caesarea called Cornelius, a centurion of the band called the Italian band, a devout man, and one that feared God **with all his house**, which gave much alms to the people, and prayed to God always....*

And now send men to Joppa, and call for one Simon, whose surname is Peter:

he lodgeth with one Simon a tanner, whose house is by the sea side: he shall tell thee what thou oughtest to do....

*While Peter yet spake these words, **the Holy Ghost fell on all them** which heard the word* (Acts 10:1-2,5-6,44).

What a day that was! Cornelius and his family received the gift of salvation and the baptism of the Holy Ghost with the evidence of speaking in other tongues. God interrupted Peter's preaching and saved the whole family. God will do the same for you. There will be some disturbances, and your family will be saved.

Timothy

We learn of Timothy from the two Epistles that Paul wrote to him. He was the pastor of the church in Ephesus. Look at the great insight that Paul gives us into the life of Timothy:

*When I call to remembrance the unfeigned faith **that is in thee, which dwelt first in thy grandmother Lois, and thy mother Eunice**; and I am persuaded that in thee also* (2 Timothy 1:5).

Here we see that Timothy was saved. His mother and his grandmother were saved. Once again we see salvation in a family.

Zacchaeus

He had three things against him—Zacchaeus was short, a chief pub-lican, and people hated him for being a thief. When he sought salva-tion, Jesus said,

>*...This day is salvation come to this house, forsomuch as he also is a son of Abraham.*

>*For the Son of man is come to seek and to save that which was lost* (Luke 19:9-10).

From these six examples, you must settle in your conscious and subconscious mind that God wants to save every member of your family. So with that settled in your spirit, how do you proceed with the salvation of your loved ones? Heaven is your destination, and it is for your family as well.

Your Responsibilities

Claim Your Rights

There is nothing automatic in the Word of God. Yes, it is true that Jesus already paid the price and shed His blood, but it is up to you to appropri-ate salvation for yourself, as well as healing and prosperity.

Lillian B. Yeoman, an old-time saint, made this statement many years ago: "God has tied himself irrevocably to human cooperation in the execution of divine purpose. He has made the faith of man a deter-mining factor in the work of redemption."

We can simply say today, "Stake your claim on what belongs to you." You do so by finding God's promises and rehearsing them to God, your-self, and the devil.

You say them to God, because He said, *"Concerning the work of My hands, command ye Me"* (Isa. 45:11b).

You say them to the devil, because the Word is the sword of the Spirit that will cut him down (see Eph. 6).

You say them to yourself, because faith comes by consistently con-fessing and hearing the Word of God (see Rom. 10:17). You must pray for your loved ones, as Paul instructed Timothy in his Epistle (see 2 Tim. 2:1-6), for salvation to come to all men. In prayer, take God's promises and declare them. We have discussed examples where God saved the families of Noah and others. Remind God of His promises. For even though God never forgets His promises, He enjoys seeing His children stand on His Word. Tell God, "If You saved Noah's family and You saved Rahab's family, then you can save my husband." Successful prayer always uses the Word and God's promises for a solid foundation.

Rebuke the Spirit of Blindness

The Gospel of Jesus Christ is so logical that it confounds us when so-called educated and so-called sensible people reject it. To remain unsaved is the most illogical thing a person can ever do. Why do people reject Christ though? The apostle Paul sheds some light on this issue:

> But if our gospel be hid, it is hid to them that are lost: in whom **the god of this world hath blinded the minds** of them which believe not, lest **the light** of the glorious gospel of Christ, who is the image of God, should shine unto them (2 Corinthians 4:3-4).

The reason your loved one is not saved yet, even after all your incessant talk and witnessing, is because your loved one is blind. No matter how powerful the light is, it does not do any good for a blind person or someone who is blindfolded. The problem is not the light, but the scales on their eyes. When the Bible says they are blind, it is not talking about optical blindness but blindness of understanding, mind, and heart.

> This I say therefore, and testify in the Lord, that ye henceforth walk not as other Gentiles walk, in the vanity of their mind,
>
> having **the understanding darkened, being alienated from the life of God** through the ignorance that is in them, **because of the blindness of their heart** (Ephesians 4:17-18).

To remove the blindness from their heart, you have to deal with the spirit of blindness. All your incessant talk, tracts under the pillow, and constant tape playing in the house, though noble, are not helping but actually causing them to rebel. The god of this world, satan, has blinded their understanding, and nothing seems to penetrate their soul. Therefore, you must go against the spirit of blindness, resist and cast him out of the lives of your loved ones. The problem is spiritual, so do not try to reason with them. Don't try to intimidate them by saying, "You have a devil, and ain't no devil staying in my house." Many have lost their loved ones for lack of wisdom. The problem is the spirit of blindness.

> *For we wrestle not against flesh and blood, but against principalities, against powers, against the rulers of the darkness of this world, against spiritual wickedness in high places* (Ephesians 6:12).

> *...Resist the devil, and he will flee from you* (James 4:7).

> *Be sober, be vigilant; because your adversary the devil, as a roaring lion, walketh about, seeking whom he may devour: whom resist stedfast in the faith...* (1 Peter 5:8-9).

> *Neither give place to the devil* (Ephesians 4:27).

Plead the Blood of Jesus

Salvation is a reality today because of the shed blood of Jesus. His blood plays an important role in the salvation of your family. Paul tells the Corinthian saints that Old Testament events and stories are for our examples and admonition today. Consider the Exodus—how were the families of Israel saved from the judgment of the angel of death?

Through the sprinkling of the shed blood on the door of the house. All those who remained in the house under the cover of the blood were saved and protected.

How was Rahab's family saved?

> *Behold, when we come into the land, thou shalt bind this line of scarlet thread in the window which thou didst let us down by: and thou shalt bring thy father, and thy mother, and thy brethren, and all thy father's household, home unto thee.*

> *And it shall be, that whosoever shall go out of the doors of thy house into the street, his blood shall be upon his head, and we will be guiltless: and whosoever shall be with thee in the house, his blood shall be on our head, if any hand be upon him* (Joshua 2:18-19).

The scarlet thread is a type and picture of the blood of Jesus. The scarlet thread hanging outside her window saved her entire family. John the revelator, tells us that we overcome satan by the blood of the Lamb and by the word of our testimony. As we have discussed, pleading the blood has nothing to do with a beggarly mentality but simply means declaring and confessing your faith in the blood of Jesus. Satan has no weapon in his arsenal that can deal with the blood. The blood of Jesus always brings the victory.

Pray for God to Send Laborers in Their Paths

Prayer will play an important role in the salvation of your family. Why? Because prayer produces fruit.

> *I exhort therefore, that,* **first of all, supplications, prayers, intercessions, and giving of thanks, be made for all men***; for kings, and for all that are in authority; that we may lead a quiet and peaceable life in all godliness and honesty.*
>
> **For this is good and acceptable in the sight of God our Saviour;**
>
> *who* **will have all men to be saved***, and to come unto the knowledge of the truth* (1 Timothy 2:1-4).

I want you to be aware of the connection between prayer and salvation. Paul reiterated this truth in his Galatian Epistle when he said, *"My little children, of whom I travail in birth again until Christ be formed in you"* (Gal. 4:19). Prayer brings birth in the Kingdom of God. Pray for your loved one that God will send laborers or witnesses in his path who will share the Gospel, and that he will not be able to resist the wisdom and anointing under which they speak. Your intercessions, prayers, and petitions are not in vain. God is still a God who answers prayer. His promise to you has not expired. He still says:

> *Call unto Me and I will answer thee...* (Jeremiah 33:3).

Have a Voice of Thanksgiving

All biblical prayers will lead to praise. In praying for your loved one's salvation, start praising the Lord for the miracle. Moaning, murmuring, and complaining do not mix with the attitude of thanksgiving. If you start praising God for the salvation of your loved one instead of griping about them, you will see quicker results. This brings us once again to the instruction that Paul gave to Timothy:

> *I exhort therefore, that, first of all, supplications, prayers, intercessions,* **and giving of thanks***, be made for all men...* (1 Timothy 2:1).

Having an attitude of gratitude is an important factor. With that kind of attitude, you will treat them as though they are already saved, and they will respond accordingly. They may kick up a fuss at first, but Jesus will always have the last word. The Bible says, *"Love never fails"* (see 1 Cor. 13). An attitude of love, praise, and thanksgiving will always defeat the devil. Do not bother to get into arguments with your loved one. It will not solve anything but only create friction between the two of you. The Scriptures clearly state, *"The wrath of man worketh not the righteousness of God"* (James 1:20). Simply live your life before them, rejoicing and maintaining your integrity. Keep a happy and joyful spirit.

> *The same goes for you wives: Be good wives to your husbands, responsive to their needs. There are husbands who, indifferent as they are to any words about God, will be captivated by your life of holy beauty* (1 Peter 3:1-2 MSG).

This Scripture works for wives, parents, brothers, and also for husbands. You have a right for your loved ones to be saved. Do not fall for the tricks and lies of satan. Jesus Christ defeated him 2,000 years ago on the cross, and the victory belongs to you.

> *Now the God of peace, that brought again from the dead our Lord Jesus, that great shepherd of the sheep, through the blood of the everlasting covenant, make you perfect in every good work to do His will, working in you that which is wellpleasing in His sight, through Jesus Christ; to whom be glory for ever and ever. Amen* (Hebrews 13:20-21).

CHAPTER 12

When Trouble Comes, Claim the Blood

These things I have spoken unto you, that in Me ye might have peace. **In the world ye shall have tribulation:** *but be of good cheer; I have overcome the world* (John 16:33).

I've told you all this so that trusting Me, you will be unshakable and assured, deeply at peace. **In this godless world you will continue to experience difficulties**. *But take heart! I've conquered the world* (John 16:33 MSG).

Notice these words from the Master's lips: "In the world ye shall have tribulation." Other versions translate the word "tribulation" as "distress," "affliction," and "pressure." One thing is for sure—if you are alive and on planet Earth, you will be tried. You have an adversary, an enemy called the devil, and he hates you. I realize that's not a nice thing to say, but nonetheless, it is a reality. Jesus said, "In the world you will have tribulation." You must understand that testings and trials come to everybody in some shape or form. They may differ in their appearance, but they all cause stress in the lives of people all over the world.

Now if you read just the first half of this verse, you would remain depressed and say, "Woe is me." But thank God, Jesus did not stop halfway but went on to say, "...but be of good cheer; I have overcome the world." He has already conquered the world, and you can do the same. The apostle John told us in His Epistle, *"As He* [Jesus] *is, so are we in this world"* (1 John 4:17). If Jesus has already overcome the world and we are like Him, then we also have overcome whatever the world will send our way. So do not be disheartened; although there will be storms, I have good news for you.

The Storms of Life

Storms of Life Come to Everyone at Some Point in Our Lives

Jesus already has warned us! So when you become a Christian, it does not mean that you will not face any problem, but God has given you weapons to destroy these problems. Other writers of the Scriptures also declare that problems will arise.

> *If thou faint **in the day of adversity**, thy strength is small* (Proverbs 24:10).

> *Wherefore take unto you the whole armour of God, that ye may be able **to withstand in the evil day**, and having done all, to stand* (Ephesians 6:13).

The book of wisdom teaches us about a day of adversity, and the apostle Paul tells us of an evil day. So one thing is for certain—trials come to all of us. I am not immune from times of testings and trials and neither are you.

The apostle Peter also reveals in his writings that times of trials will come:

> *Beloved, **think it not strange concerning the fiery trial** which is to try you, **as though some strange thing happened unto you*** (1 Peter 4:12).

> *Dear friends, do not be surprised at finding that that scorching flame of persecution is raging among you to put you to the test—as though some surprising thing were accidentally happening to you* (1 Peter 4:12 WNT).

What Jesus, Solomon, Peter, and Paul are saying is to not ever be surprised by anything. In other words, always be ready and stand your guard to fight and win.

You Cannot Prevent the Storms of Life From Coming, but You Can Determine Their Outcome

Problems, difficulties, and pressures will come, but I do not have to collapse underneath them as a helpless victim. Even the Lord Jesus went through a storm as recorded in the Gospels, but He did not collapse, faint, or die in the storm.

"Oh, but Brother Glenn, He was the Son of God!"

And so are you.

"Yeah, but He was anointed with the Holy Spirit."

And so are you.

"Yeah, but He walked in authority and power."

And so can you.

There are no excuses! Those who makes excuses will excuse themselves from the greatness that God has for them.

You can determine the outcome of the storms of life just as Jesus did. Remember, Jesus is the author of our faith. You never read in your Bible that when Jesus was in the storm, He started running around on the deck of the boat, screaming and yelling, "Oh My God, we are doomed! Oh My God, we are all going to die!" You never heard it from Jesus, and you never heard it from the apostle Paul when he was in a storm at sea. Notice what Paul actually said:

> *But after long abstinence Paul stood forth in the midst of them, and said, Sirs, ye should have hearkened unto me, and not have loosed from Crete, and to have gained this harm and loss.*
>
> ***And now I exhort you to be of good cheer****: for there shall be no loss of any man's life among you, but of the ship.*
>
> *For there stood by me this night the angel of God, whose I am, and whom I serve, saying, Fear not, Paul; thou must be brought before Caesar: and, lo, God hath given thee all them that sail with thee.*
>
> *Wherefore,* **sirs, be of good cheer: for I believe God, that it shall be even as it was told me** (Acts 27:21-25).

While everybody was giving up and waiting for death, Paul had victory on his mind. He changed the outcome of his storm as did Jesus, and so can you. I like what the apostle Paul said, "…it shall be even as it was told me." Can you see here that Paul believed the report of the Lord and determined to change the outcome of this deadly storm? If Paul did it, so can you.

If Daniel could escape the lion's mouth, so can you.

If Meshach, Shadrach and Abednego could escape the fiery furnace, so can you.

In the first chapter of the Book of Philippians, when Paul was thrust into prison, he did not lose hope but boldly declared:

For I know that this shall turn to my salvation… (Philippians 1:19).

For I know that this will turn out for my deliverance… (Philippians 1:19 NAS).

Paul determined and declared his victory. He was a man who determined the final outcome of the storm. Satan started it, but Paul had the last word. Never give the devil the last word. If you do, he will determine the final outcome, and it most assuredly will be failure and defeat. As long as Israel permitted Goliath to speak, he held them in fear and captivity. David, however, did not allow Goliath to have the last word; consequently, David won the battle. Once you have been walking with God for some time, you will discover that satan loves to talk. And the more you entertain him, the more fear and lies he will inject into your mind. After Goliath finished speaking, David did not stay quiet and meditate upon what Goliath said, but he instead declared:

Then said David to the Philistine, *Thou comest to me with a sword, and with a spear, and with a shield: but I come to thee in the name of the Lord of hosts, the God of the armies of Israel, whom thou hast defied.*

This day will the Lord deliver thee into mine hand; *and I will smite thee, and take thine head from thee; and I will give the carcases of the host of the Philistines this day unto the fowls of the air, and to the wild beasts of the earth; that all the earth may know that there is a God in Israel.*

And all this assembly shall know that the Lord saveth not with sword and spear: for the battle is the Lord's, and He will give you into our hands (1 Samuel 17:45-47).

In the natural, Goliath was bigger and stronger, but David still determined the outcome of the battle.

The Storms of Life Will Reveal the Real You

Many of us are legends in our own minds. We think we are stronger than what we really are. Then when a storm comes along, we fall apart. So many people give the appearance that they have got it all together but as soon as adverse circumstances arise against them, they wither under the pressure and you soon see what they are made up of—which was not much.

If thou faint in the day of adversity, thy strength is small (Proverbs 24:10).

If you fall to pieces in a crisis, there wasn't much to you in the first place (Proverbs 24:10 MSG).

If you fail under pressure, your strength is not very great (Proverbs 24:10 New Living Translation).

I really like The Message translation's rendering: "If you fall to pieces in a crisis, there wasn't much to you in the first place." Wow! What an indictment. Fainting and falling apart in a crisis reveals how strong you really are, or how weak you really are. I also like the way the Good News Bible translates this verse: "If you are weak in a crisis, you are weak indeed." Make it your ultimate goal in life to be strong in the Lord so that you do not collapse in the day of adversity.

With these three primary understandings having been addressed, let us find out what to do when trouble comes. We will use Paul's instruction to the Philippian church as our mode of operation.

How to React When Trouble Comes

No Sign of Fear

And in nothing terrified by your adversaries: which is to them an evident token of perdition, but to you of salvation, and that of God (Philippians 1:28).

151

And in nothing affrighted by the adversaries: which is for them an evident token of perdition, but of your salvation, and that from God (Philippians 1:28 ASV).

...not flinching or dodging in the slightest before the opposition... (Philippians 1:28 MSG).

The moment trouble hits, fear wants to get a foothold in your heart. Yet Paul said not to show any sign of fear. Do not flinch. Make up your mind, "No fear here." Fear will cripple your faith and will rob you of your victory. It will terrorize you. But freedom from fear and terror is your inheritance. There is no need for the people of God to be afraid. Fear is not natural for a child of God. When you were born again, you did not receive the spirit of fear but the spirit of faith.

For ye have not received the spirit of bondage again to fear; but ye have received the Spirit of adoption, whereby we cry, Abba, Father. The Spirit itself beareth witness with our spirit, that we are the children of God (Romans 8:15-16).

Fear is the spirit of bondage, but God does not want you in bondage. There is nothing good about fear. Somebody will say, "Well, what about the fear of the Lord?" That is totally different. The fear of the Lord simply means respect, awesome reverence, and obedience to Him. It does not mean that I am afraid of God hurting me. God is not my problem, but my solution.

God's people should not be coping with fear or learning about fear management. No! We should be attacking it. Fear is not your inheritance; it is your enemy because it is not from God.

For God hath not given us the spirit of fear; but of power, and of love, and of a sound mind (2 Timothy 1:7).

If God did not give it to you, then you should not be tolerating it in your life. If God did not give it to you, then you have a right to cast it out. If God did not give it to you, then it should be abnormal to you. A believer must treat fear just like sin. No tolerance! You must resist all kinds of fears. The following fears are not normal, and they will rob you of a life of victory.

◆ Fear of death.

◆ Fear of satan.

- ◆ Fear of sicknesses.
- ◆ Fear of the past.
- ◆ Fear of the present.
- ◆ Fear of the future.
- ◆ Fear of flying.
- ◆ Fear of men.
- ◆ Fear of failure.
- ◆ Fear of success.

All of the above are not your inheritance. You have been called to a life of power and victory.

> *Have not I commanded thee? Be strong and of a good courage; be not afraid, neither be thou dismayed: for the Lord thy God is with thee whithersoever thou goest* (Joshua 1:9).

> *For God hath not given us the spirit of fear; but of power, and of love, and of a sound mind* (2 Timothy 1:7).

Fear is not normal for the believer, and you should never walk in fear. Any form of fear should be firmly dealt with. A fear-free life can be a reality in your life. And there are six indelible reasons why you can live a fear-free life.

1. You can live above fear because it is not from God.

   > *For God hath not given us the spirit of fear; but of power, and of love, and of a sound mind* (2 Timothy 1:7).

2. Fear has no hold over you because you live in a different Kingdom.

   > *Giving thanks unto the Father, which hath made us meet to be partakers of the inheritance of the saints in light: who hath delivered us from the power of darkness, and hath translated us into the kingdom of His dear Son* (Colossians 1:12-13).

3. Fear has to find an exit when faith walks in.

   > *For whatsoever is born of God overcometh the world: and this is the victory that overcometh the world, even our faith* (1 John 5:4).

4. God is with you.

Have not I commanded thee? Be strong and of a good courage; be not afraid, neither be thou dismayed: **for the Lord thy God is with thee whithersoever thou goest** (Joshua 1:9).

Let your conversation be without covetousness; and be content with such things as ye have: **for He hath said, I will never leave thee, nor forsake thee. So that we may boldly say, The Lord is my helper, and I will not fear what man shall do unto me** (Hebrew 13:5-6).

5. God is for you.

What shall we then say to these things? If God be for us, who can be against us? (Romans 8:31).

The Lord is on my side; I will not fear: what can man do unto me? (Psalm 118:6).

I, even I, am He that comforteth you: who art thou, that thou shouldest be afraid of a man that shall die, and of the son of man which shall be made as grass*; and forgettest the Lord thy maker, that hath stretched forth the heavens, and laid the foundations of the earth; and hast feared continually every day because of the fury of the oppressor, as if he were ready to destroy? and where is the fury of the oppressor?* (Isaiah 51:12-13).

6. God is in me.

To whom God would make known what is the riches of the glory of this mystery among the Gentiles; which is Christ in you, the hope of glory (Colossians 1:27).

For in Him dwelleth all the fulness of the Godhead bodily (Colossians 2:9).

Control Your Emotions

One of the hardest things to do when trouble is at your door is to control your emotions. There are positive emotions and there are negative ones. Your emotions are a result of your thinking. If you want to control your emotions, you have to control what you allow your mind to entertain. What you ponder upon or meditate on will determine your emotions. You do not want to dwell on the negatives that will give you a sense of despondency and despair. For this reason I do not call everybody under the sun when I am facing a critical situation. The more you rehearse your problems to people, the more despondent you become. Besides, you do not know a person's philosophy or ethos. In the back of someone's mind, they could be thinking, *You deserve this trial; it is the judgment of God.* In another person's thinking could be, *Maybe God has sent this trial in your life to teach you something.* All of these reasonings are not right. When trouble comes, you have to take control over the thoughts of your mind and bring them to the obedience of God's Word. Satan will inject all kinds of images in your mind to nullify your faith and courage. And with these pictures bombarding your mind, there will be the tendency to cry, fall apart, and get emotional. And you cannot afford to do that, for satan is looking for just a hint of fear so that he knows when to pounce. Fear, doubt, paranoia, and unbelief are to satan what blood is to a shark. The moment he sniffs or sees it, he moves swiftly to destroy his victim.

Lisa's Finger

When my daughter, Lisa, was 6 years old, she had an accident in church, where her little finger was crushed in a door. After rushing her to the hospital, staff said there was nothing they could do about the finger, which was just hanging by the skin, and it would have to come off. When my wife heard this news in the hospital, she began to turn red and was about to faint. I looked at her and said sternly, "No, you don't! I do not have time to deal with you now. If you want to get emotional, do it after we get the victory. Right now we are working on a miracle." There was blood everywhere, and as I mentioned, I do not like the sight of blood. I could have become queasy and dizzy, but I held my emotions. Satan kept showing me images of my daughter with one finger missing, and in the natural, I wanted to yelp, "Oh my baby! Oh my Lord! Do something!" Instead, I held and controlled my emotions until I got the victory. Even when they were saying there was nothing they could do, I said to myself, "God will heal my baby's finger." And today, she is perfectly well and her finger is totally fine.

Everybody has emotions, but controlling them is absolutely vital to winning the battle. I realize that time and discipline are needed, but you cannot afford to quiver as satan will pounce on you the moment you show weakness. Do not let your emotions have the best of you. To be emotional in a situation is to be governed by a feeling or sentiment rather than sound reasoning, which is the result of constant meditation on the Word of God, which in turn, will produce courage and the right emotions. Paul tells us in Hebrews:

> *Cast not away therefore your confidence, which hath great recompence of reward.*
>
> *For ye have need of patience, that, after ye have done the will of God, ye might receive the promise* (Hebrews 10:35-36).

You maintain your confidence by trusting what you know of God and relying on your knowledge of the promises of God. He will never break His Word. As long as you stay in confidence, you will be rewarded. God said so and it will be so in your life.

Voice Your Faith, Not Your Fear or Frailty

If you control what is in your mind, what comes out of your mouth will already be determined. Your mouth is a reflection of your mind. When trouble comes, you need to voice your faith and not your frustrations.

> *And they overcame him by the blood of the Lamb, and by the word of their testimony...* (Revelation 12:11).
>
> *And they overcame him because of the blood of the Lamb and because of the word of their testimony...* (Revelation 12:11 NAS).

Notice one of the reasons we defeat satan is because of the word of our testimony. I like to say it this way, "And they overcame satan because of the blood and because of the voicing of their faith." In the Greek translation, this verse is rendered as, "And they overcame satan because of the blood of the Lamb and because of their testifying the sayings of God." Voicing what God has said about us is crucial and essential in order to win over troubled times. Your voice is a result of your thoughts, and when God's Word sculptures your thoughts, they become faith-filled. It is important for you to note that your words will determine the atmosphere and outcome of a circumstance.

> *Death and life are in the power of the tongue: and they that love it shall eat the fruit thereof* (Proverbs 18:21).

Your voice is your sound system. In fact, every person who has ever lived on God's earth has been subject to the power of his or her own tongue. The Bible declares that there is power in our tongue. You can add life or death by what proceeds out of your mouth.

As believers, it is our duty to speak the Word of God and voice our faith. The voicing of your faith is the voicing of your confidence in the ability of God to deliver in the midst of adverse circumstances. The Word was not given to you for it to stay on your coffee table. The purpose of the Word is for you to speak it. Your victory over devils and circumstances is in the voicing of the promises of God.

And they overcame him by the blood of the Lamb, and by the word of their testimony... (Revelation 12:11).

The decrees of God that are spoken in faith will dominate and conquer all the works of the devil. You have to realize that you are a king and your commands matter.

Where *the word of a king is,* **there** *is power: and who may say unto him, What doest thou?* (Ecclesiastes 8:4).

Thou shalt also decree a thing, and it shall be established unto thee: and the light shall shine upon thy ways (Job 22:28).

There is power where the king voices his word. Whatever you say in a circumstance becomes a decree that works for or against you. Therefore, you have to hold fast to your confession of God's promises.

Pray in the Spirit

I do not know how people can live without the turbo boost of praying in the Spirit. What do I mean by the term "praying in the Spirit"? I understand that many claim that all prayers are prayed in the Spirit, but the Scriptures unmistakably call praying in tongues the language of the Spirit.

For he that speaketh in an **unknown tongue** *speaketh not unto men, but unto God: for no man understandeth him; howbeit* **in the spirit** *he speaketh mysteries* (1 Corinthians 14:2).

This verse is not in reference to giving a message in tongues, which would be from God to the people; rather, this verse is talking about praying in tongues, which is going upwards whereas a message in tongues is downwards. The apostle Paul who faced death on numerous occasions had a very interesting thought on the subject of tongues.

I thank my God, I speak with tongues more than ye all (1 Corinthians 14:18).

In my mind, the ability to pray in tongues is one of the best gifts that God has given to the believer. There are many benefits, but I want to give you just seven reasons why it is absolutely vital for you to pray in the Spirit when trouble comes. Remember, praying in the Spirit is synonymous with praying in tongues.

1. *When you pray in tongues, it is a source of spiritual edification charging you up like a battery.* When trouble comes, it wants to sap you of your energy, courage, and zeal; but praying in the Spirit will keep the flame burning.

   He that speaketh in an unknown tongue edifieth himself (1 Corinthians 14:4a).

2. *When you pray in tongues, it is your direct line to God.* When trouble comes, you need to have an audience with God. He is your best contact.

   For he that speaketh in an unknown tongue, speaketh not unto men but unto God...(1 Corinthians 14:2).

3. *When you pray in tongues, it will build and stimulate your faith.* Faith is what overcomes the world, and when trouble comes, you need all the faith you can get to remove mountains and walk on the sea.

   But ye, beloved, building up yourselves on your most holy faith, praying in the Holy Ghost (Jude 20).

   But you, beloved, **build yourselves up** [founded] *on your most holy faith* [make progress, rise like an edifice higher and higher], **praying in the Holy Spirit** (Jude 20 Amplified Bible).

4. *When you pray in tongues, you are operating instantly in the realm of the Spirit.* This is the place where miracles and the supernatural become realities. From the realm of the Spirit, you can dominate the natural world. You will be operating from a higher realm dominating the lower realm.

   For he that speaketh in an unknown tongue speaketh not unto men, but unto God: for no man understandeth him; howbeit in the spirit he speaketh mysteries (1 Corinthians 14:2).

5. *When you pray in tongues, you pray the perfect will of God for the situation.* Sometimes when trouble comes, we do not know

how to effectively pray from our mind. It might be a case of insufficient information or too much information, but nevertheless, when you pray in tongues, the Spirit of God will guide your prayer.

Likewise the Spirit also helpeth our infirmities: for we know not what we should pray for as we ought: but the Spirit itself maketh intercession for us with groanings which cannot be uttered.

And He that searcheth the hearts knoweth what is the mind of the Spirit, because He maketh intercession for the saints according to the will of God.

And we know that all things work together for good to them that love God, to them who are the called according to His purpose (Romans 8:26-28).

6. *When you pray in tongues, you will be refreshed and receive rest from the Holy Ghost.* Situations of life can make us battle weary. It may not just be physical tiredness but also mental tiredness or spiritual drain. When you pray in the Holy Ghost, you will be refreshing yourself with the rivers of living water.

*For with **stammering lips and another tongue** will He speak to this people.*

To whom He said, This is the rest wherewith ye may cause the weary to rest; and this is the refreshing… (Isaiah 28:11-12).

7. *When you pray in tongues, God will give you impressions and the answer to your problem.* Ideas and perception come when you pray in tongues. That is one of the major ways God speaks to us today in order to deliver us. I encourage you to pray in the Spirit daily, it will make you sensitive to the voice of God.

Hold the Bloodline

God is the same! The Word is the same! The answer is the same! In an ever-changing world, it is comforting to know some things remain the same. The bloodline from the beginning has always protected those who have exercised faith in it. Moses and all of Israel believed in the bloodline over their house to protect them from the death angel. The children of Israel had a blood defense, and so do we. Continue to hold the bloodline by applying it through the confession of the blood and the

Word in prayer. Keep your mind on God's Word and expect the battle to turn in your favor. The blood still works today! Victory is yours.

They overcame him by the blood of the Lamb and by the word of their testimony.

CONTACT THE AUTHOR

Glenn Arekion Ministries

PO Box 72672
Louisville, KY 40272
USA

mail@glennarekion.org
www.glennarekion.org

Another exciting title from
GLENN AREKION

SEVEN WAYS TO INCREASE YOUR ANOINTING
by *Glenn Arekion*

*What you are about to read will revolutionize your life
and take you to a higher dimension!*

The anointing is the most indispensable force in the life of the believer. With it, you will have the power and faith to do great exploits. Without it, life and ministry will be a constant source of frustration and irritation. Many have visions but simply do not know how to make them realities in their lives.

The pages of this book are full of answers to your most frustrating questions. The name of the game is results, and when you know how to purposely tap into the anointing and treasures of God, you will:

- Be transformed into a different person.
- Be elevated into a new place in God.
- Be the catalyst for positive change in the lives of suffering people.
- See your dream become your destiny.

Seven Ways to Increase Your Anointing will answer your heart's cry. It will show you how to remove the powerlessness and lack of influence in your life, while empowering you to do the mighty works of God.

ISBN: 978-88-89127-84-1

Additional copies of this book and other book
titles from DESTINY IMAGE EUROPE
are available at your local bookstore.

We are adding new titles every month!

To view our complete catalog online, visit us at:
www.eurodestinyimage.com

Send a request for a catalog to:

**Via Acquacorrente, 6
65123 - Pescara - ITALY
Tel. +39 085 4716623 - Fax +39 085 9431270**

"Changing the world, one book at a time."

Are you an author?

Do you have a "today" God-given message?

CONTACT US

We will be happy to review your manuscript
for the possibility of publication:

publisher@eurodestinyimage.com
http://www.eurodestinyimage.com/pages/AuthorsAppForm.htm